PRAISE FOR WH

"I couldn't put Ann's manuscript down once I started to read it. She truly speaks to the heart and soul of her readers, and I am proud to be able to say that she is a Today's Caregiver magazine Caregiver Friendly Award winner, as well for her other book, "Joy-Full Journaling for the Caregiver's Spirit: A Transformational Workbook." Everyone needs to read Ann's books."

—**Gary Edward Barg**, CEO
Editor-In-Chief
Caregiver Media Group
Empowering Fearless Caregivers since 1995
Today's Caregiver magazine
Fearless Caregiver Conferences
Caregiver Friendly Awards

ॐ

"Ann E. Agueli has done it again! Each time she touches pen to paper, I swear she leaves the world a little better than she found it. In When God Nods, Agueli weaves together stories of faith, synchronicity and enlightenment, evoking inspiration with the turn of each and every page. She takes the reader on an insightful journey and shows us how to discover the blessing in each lesson we uncover along the way. A heartfelt read filled with God's love and grace!"

—**Shanda Trofe**, Bestselling author of *Authorpreneur*
and *Write from the Heart*, President & CEO
of Transcendent Publishing

"As an author and student of life, I am constantly seeking wisdom and stories of hope that raise my awareness about spirituality. Ann's book, "When God Nods" will deepen your faith and open your eyes to the greater plans that God has designed in your life. While our stories are often messy, complicated, and imperfect, Ann reminds us that we can find our grace and purpose by bringing our faith to everyday experiences. Although it is human nature to try to figure out everything, Ann advises the reader to trust that a higher plan is always unfolding and collaborate with God. This book will reaffirm that we are always enough and our struggles along the way will strengthen us by teaching us about humility and compassion. By the end of her story you'll understand why fear can hold us back in our lives and it can get in the way of building a powerful relationship with God. If you are soul seeking..... this book is a gift for you."

—**Krista Gawronski**
Founder of Fabulous Women of Sonoma County
Author of Soul Purpose...Finding The Courage to Fly

&

"When GOD Nods~is a Spiritual Free Transforming JOURNEY! This remarkable gathering of short stories, Ann touches our HEARTS through her gift of tender enlightening storytelling. It's feels like - Ann is sitting beside you, as your read through the freestyle painting of the pages. The way the stories flows and the REVERANCE of GOD that is channeled through Ann ~ is a true testament to her Purpose. She has the gift of gently extracting the essence of each story ! The Divine Serendipity that has soulfully evolved is HUMBLING !"

—**ReneMarie**, Language of Love Foundation Inc.

When God Nods

Inspirational Tales of Divine Serendipity

Uncover the Lesson
And Discover the Blessing

ANN E. AGUELI

When God Nods

Inspirational Tales of Divine Serendipity

Uncover the Lesson And Discover the Blessing

These stories are, as told to by, with permission from the subjects in accordance to their recollection, point-of-view, and perceptions.

My stories are from my own personal experiences, recollection, point-of-view, and perceptions according to my experience and memories of them.

Published by

Transcendent Publishing
PO Box 66202
St. Pete Beach, FL 33706
www.transcendentpublishing.com

ISBN-10: 0-9982869-1-5
ISBN-13: 978-0-9982869-1-4

Printed in the United States of America.

DEDICATION

To all the divine souls living in human beings because we all
have divinity within

First and foremost, to God for continuing to nod at me even
when He probably wanted to shake his head

To my children: I am so blessed and so proud. Each one of you
desires to be a contribution and

make a difference in this world

To my parents: For waiting on God's promise to have me

To my soul tribe: You know who you are and how much I
honor and adore you

To my lessons and for the ability to turn them into blessings.

So be it (Amen).

ACKNOWLEDGEMENTS

To my three biggest blessings, my children Ralph, Julianna, and Annalesa; God has graced me abundantly with your presence; you are all beyond amazing.

In memory of my Mom who just passed away,

To God for the coincidences and serendipities,

For angels seen and unseen, and

To the life lessons which turned into life's blessings.

CONTENTS

INTRODUCTION

Have you ever had a coincidence where you looked over your shoulder in hopes someone else witnessed or heard what you just experienced? You know the kind – where it could only have come from God or a message from your angels? It is no accident that you are reading this right now either.

What you are about to engage in is a collection of stories where serendipity and divinity intertwine – true stories of serendipitous accounts with people who were open to the thought consciousness of a higher being whose name is God. It is my intention through this writing to offer inspiring stories of connection; some are astonishing while others are quite humorous, but all will leave you feeling emotionally motivated, inspired, and hopefully, led down a different path. That path is the path to euphoric enlightenment. You will gain insight on how to learn the lesson and discover – or rather uncover – the blessings by reading other people's tales of divine serendipity.

Once I stood up and showed up, took responsibility for my life and partnered with God, the miracles began to occur at the speed of light. It would make my heart sing for you to receive this same experience.

For me, the greatest thing about my life, my personal experience, is that I get to create it as I go along; there are no rights, no wrongs, just the ever-forward, constant and continuous motion of forward movement. Changing direction is nothing to be ashamed of; it's simply part of the process of uncovering who you are and who you wish to be.

i

As long as I show up as who I truly am, allowing my mask to fall to the ground, there's nothing wrong. Show up as who you truly are and all things will come into alignment with who you are meant to be. Try on new things, take a challenge, be courageous, and if it does not work out, who cares. Exploring different things means you are courageous enough to explore yourself.

Following the light is not something for the deceased; it is for the living. Once you discover, or rather uncover that light, you will be compelled to move toward it each and every day. It will be like the pull of the moon against the tide. You will come to know it as part of your "self," but outside of your "self." It is akin to walking down a path with no compass and no set direction. It is a following where thinking is not a big part of the process, but being and flowing are the process itself.

She extended her hand and said,
"Hi God, I'm Ann."

He responded, "I know who you are,
but do you know who I am?"

CHAPTER ONE
BITS AND PIECES OF MY SILLY HUMAN STUFF

Sometimes I think God has a watch and He looks at it, shakes His head and taps His foot waiting for me. He waits for me to make up my mind. He waits for me to align with His will. He waits for me to be quiet and to "get" the message! For those who know me (and love me), they know I have quite the energetic mind.

Sometimes I think God also mutters to Himself, "Why, oh why did I give her such a busy, active mind? Must she always analyze every little thing?" As I picture this vision, I laugh out loud. Instead of referring to myself as "stubborn," I like to say I am, "Fiercely Determined." So, determined, that nothing else but transformation would do.

Once I consciously sought out transformation, the rest fell into alignment – none of it was easy, but I wouldn't change a thing – not even the hard stuff; most especially not the hard stuff.

It was there in the space of hardship at the corner of difficult and "really???" where I learned and grew. Growing pains hurt, but when you do something good, good comes back to you. When you make a poor choice, you experience the repercussions of those choices, so you can improve next time around. And, if not, then the time after that – until you "get" it. There's nothing "bad" about your life journey, only choices. Each of those choices gets you one step closer to being who you were truly meant to be, if you are willing to learn the lesson and uncover the blessing.

God has a way of guiding you, ever so subtly and in partnership with you. You can trust Him; He is the most perfect of tour guides. He knows the route better than you do and before you do. Those unchartered territories? No worries, He's waiting at the other end. We are all aware of the peaks and valleys of life. Along with majestic views, there are some pretty steep potholes we manage to step in, too. However, it's how we perceive all those twists, turns, and roadblocks that make a difference.

When my transformation began, I didn't know yet that my subconscious was already becoming aware and my spirit was waiting to be born, getting into position, exuberant about heading toward the light; an unbelievable life was about to be born.

That life is available for you, as well. All you have to do is be a little out of your mind. No, not literally, but figuratively. Get ready to travel out of your head and journey into the depths of your heart.

CHAPTER TWO
WHAT IS A TRIAL WITHOUT A TRIUMPH? WHAT IS A STORY, IF NOT SHARED?

My Pain: Your Gain

My broken life – if it can be an example and help one person – then it will have been a life well-lived. My book, *"When God Nods,"* is so much more than another story about coincidence; it's about partnership with God.

It's about when to give up – not in the form of defeat – but giving it all up to God wholeheartedly. When you lay yourself down at God's feet at your most broken point, His mercy covers you. He will fill you up. You come to Him empty and broken and there is only one chore for Him to do, which is to restore you and fill you up through beautiful, divine transformation.

When you have nothing left to give, give it up –

to Him.

The next step is how to partner your life with God and tap into your divinity within. You get to start from nothing. Just as God created the universe from nothing, He can recreate you from nothing, as well. It's a great place to start. In partnership, you will reach your highest self.

When out on the sea of life, God will take care of the weather while you take control of the boat; choose faith.

Do you remember when you were a child playing a game outdoors and suddenly one of your friends shouted, "Do Over?" You granted them their request. When you want it, it's yours for the asking – the "Do Over" of your life. Ask and you shall receive.

When your life isn't working, God will work in your life; just believe.

You have to be open to receive. There will be trials transformed into triumphs, signs, serendipities, and coincidences. This is how you know, "*When God Nods.*"

When you first begin your journey, don't be surprised as He rips your old limiting beliefs out of you from their darkest of roots. Also, don't be surprised as you hang on to those old, familiar beliefs as you scream, cry, and thrash about wanting to hold on for dear life to everything old and familiar.

Imagine the old roots embedded for decades being pulled out of you from your inner being as your human self tries to hang on to those dangling roots for dear life. Those roots are all you have known, but they are no longer serving your tree to flourish. They are roots grounding you in fear.

"Do not conform to the patterns of this world, but be transformed by the renewing of your mind. Then you will be able to test and approve what God's will is – his good, pleasing, and perfect will." Romans 12:2 (NIV)

It is in the letting go where the journey of your best self and highest life is about to unfold. Letting go of the old as you embrace the new is the bridge to transformation.

In my book, there are tales of divine serendipity; true stories of how others experienced this divine serendipity. Are they special or unique or different from you? No way. They are exactly like you. More importantly, you can have these same experiences too. My book will also highlight, how to uncover the lessons and discover the blessings as you begin your journey across the bridge of transformation.

Intertwined with these heartfelt interviews of experiencing divine serendipities, is my story. For three years and up until present date, I have had extraordinary coincidences where I had to choose between faith and fear, where I got knocked down time and again and came back swinging and sometimes I just laid down and cried. I had work to do.

Some of the more painful coincidences were lessons I, unfortunately, needed to learn – and believe me when I say I had to learn them the hard way. This was most especially true in my repeating patterns with the same types of men – men that were not good for me personally, but I attracted them just the same.

What I didn't know then, I know now, as I look over my shoulder with a sheepish grin. I had a "victim" mentality. I was a victim of men, a victim of circumstance, and a victim of life. No more, I tell you, since my transformation. This was the hardest and most painful journey. Just as a baby grows and shapes in the womb and born into the light, and as a butterfly must leave the safety of its cocoon to emerge more beautiful than ever, you and I have the same opportunity to reach, shape, and grow.

It's time to get out of your mind, open up your heart space and, most importantly, follow the unforeseen thread connecting you to the divine. If you are like me, you may have seen 111 or 1111 pop up frequently. Here's the most "divine" 11:1 I can offer you.

"Now faith is the substance of things hoped for, the evidence of things not seen." Hebrews 11:1 (Kings James Bible)

Just listen with your spirit and turn down those voices in your mind,

"When God Nods"

Let the serendipities begin.

CHAPTER THREE
THE POWER OF DECLARATION: SHE MAY HAVE CANCER, BUT CANCER DOESN'T HAVE HER

The only certainty in these moments was uncertainty itself.

It was 2005 and she was diagnosed; it was also the year and the moment she went on a mission. She had questions, but not your typical questions of "Why Me?" Her questions were more of a spiritual kind: "What do I do next, what do I do to get this over with and finished?" She took on an attitude of this being just something to get taken care of. She was going to move on and she wasn't going to let it get her! She said today with probably as much determination as she had back then, "I wasn't going to let it bring me down or stop me from living my life."

It was a big wakeup call in the life of a middle-aged woman, according to her. She woke up from some kind of trance she believed she was in all the years preceding the diagnosis. Only thing is, she didn't know it until the moment she was diagnosed.

Her first experience was, as she recants, wondering if she could continue life as "normal" while she was going through chemo. However, "normal" was about to take on a new definition for her. Guess what? She didn't allow it to. She kept the most sense of normalcy she felt she could. Even though she was facing something so frightening, she made everything so normal. That's what she wanted; not for herself, but for her kids.

This beautiful, spiritual woman basically had some kind of awakening, which allowed her to take on a new set of lenses; it actually helped her in some strange sense of the way. She always tells people that God gave her a smack in the face and said "Wake up girl, I'm giving you a second chance and what are you going to do with it?"

For her personally, it is viewed as a gift somehow. She does tell people this all the time. Even though she did have breast cancer, so much good came out of it. When you hear the word cancer you automatically hear "You could be dying." That's the first association that came into her head because of the reputation that cancer has; you get cancer and it's going to kill you. This soul sister, however, likes to show people she's still here and it didn't kill her. She truly believes she's here to show others how it showed up as a gift (to her), which made her open up more to people about cancer.

She was starting to talk about it more; letting people know she is a survivor is when she realized she can help instead of being a victim. She took on the role of being empowered instead of cowering. Her first powerful and moving experience where she knew she wasn't going to let cancer get her was when she did her two-day walk for breast cancer. Walking 35 miles in 2 days, crossing that finish line, she said to herself with the utmost feeling of satisfaction she ever felt before - she did it! She stomped over that finish line, somehow as if she had stomped on cancer itself. More importantly she had a message for cancer. What was that message? "F You Cancer!"

She was feeling the joyful and exuberating feeling of walking over the finish line. There are no words, adjectives or descriptions which could clearly describe the feelings of being jubilant, exhilarated, and accomplished as she got closer and closer to stepping foot over that finish line. It was pure joy. It was radiant light. She glowed because she was making a statement. She always wanted to fundraise for something and there it was. The opportunity came to her. While it may have come in an unwanted and unexpected way, it still came nonetheless.

On the final day of the walk, she basically made a statement; not only for her but for those who would come after her. "Cancer you ain't gonna beat me!" This was God working in her life. She always had the desire to be a contribution; and there within the midst of a mess was the answer to her prayer to be a contribution.

God always uses her, she says humbly. This was the biggest way. She believes God puts her in places where she needs to be with people. She says you don't realize at any given moment someone needs you right there, in that moment, space, and time. She loves helping whether it's as simple as a smile or asking someone how they are, or even a hug. Her co-workers have dubbed her the best hugger around; she is a very good hugger at work, she giggles humbly. Sometimes you just need a hug; no words; she gives out hugs for no reason.

Or it could be as big as going with a friend for her mammography or sonogram because they got called back due to something suspicious showing up on the previous scan. So she had the experience to go along with a friend to get her screening on a call back. This was another life-altering event for her.

How was it life-altering? There was no way to know the outcome. The only certainty in these moments were uncertainty itself. How unsettling yet truthful this statement is. This experience, however, made her feel like a doer and a contribution. She did what needed to be done at the moment.

One day on the soccer field she began chatting up the mom of one of her daughter's friends. Without missing a beat, after hearing this woman tell her tale of fear and angst and having walked down the path of worry and fright herself, she opened up her mouth and simply said, she would go with this woman to her testing. The woman gave her a look as if she didn't believe her, but she held steadfast. "What time is the appointment because we're going together?"

The waiting is the one of the worst feelings; the not knowing how, when or if you're entire world will unfold is unnerving at best. She had the feeling of being happy when the results came in and all was well. You were happy to have the privilege to be there for someone in the moment of need, you were overjoyed to extend yourself in this manner, and elated to be there in case she needed any kind of comforting.

Bumping into this woman on the soccer field, who was her fellow sister and a fellow mom, and finding out she had a diagnosis of cancer, as well – there's no such thing as a coincidence. She truly felt she was where she was supposed to be - in the right place at the right time so God could use her. God found a way. Through heartache and triumph, this cancer survivor was able to use her experience and pull from her inner divinity and share her strength with other fellow sisters who are, unfortunately, going down the same path and through the same journey.

She has an important message and relates it to an experience she had as a Weight Watcher's Consultant. While she was working there, she noticed a tethered thread for some of these women. She'll never forget weighing people in and their choice of words. There was always a story running in the background. They used the word "hope" in a different way than she had to learn to use it. Her philosophy as long as she was recovering was "There's always hope." These women, however, would say things like they hope they wouldn't gain the weight back; almost as if inviting the weight to come on back in.

What you fear may appear or what you resist persists.

Sometimes people use the word hope, only to hope something negative doesn't happen. For her, however, she learned a new meaning and an entirely new definition for the word hope. You don't hope for something bad not to happen, you hope for something great to occur.

> ### *You don't hope for something bad not to happen, you hope for something great to occur.*

You talk to people, she reminisces, and they are either a cancer survivor or going through cancer at the moment. She was like a magnet for women experiencing cancer – a good magnet, however.

Who knows better what you're going through than the person going through it. Fortunately for her, she didn't wait to follow up with what she knew could be serious. This is another part of her important message. Don't wait, don't hesitate; follow through on any sneaking suspicion because early detection is key.

She completely understands the feeling and remembers it fiercely upon first hearing the word cancer. She also knows what chemo feels like. However, in the midst of it all, she truly feels her energy drew her to and magnetized her toward people who are in need of comfort. She was more than happy and humble to allow God to use her in this divine and selfless way.

In her heart of hearts, she owns a knowing of her own journey - God gave her this experience in order for her to be a contribution and a comfort. She went through it, and whether another soul sister was in need of a hug or had the desire to vent and talk, she was available. In humility she humbly states, "I don't have the answers but I do have the experience."

"I don't have the answers but I do have the experience."

In her humility, she adopted the attitude there was some kind of divine experience going on in the midst of something really awful. Amazingly, she was never bitter, but did have the awareness of an immediate awakening. Where did she get her supernatural connection? From early childhood, she was always close to God since she was a little girl - a little girl of only 8-years-old who walked into church by herself because she always loved the presence of God. Even until today, she still feels connected to the presence of God when she walks into a church.

She wants to tell other women what was the blessing about being diagnosed and the way she carried herself. The blessing (not only then but still now) is – just to appreciate everything so much more after being diagnosed. During treatment, she didn't really think about anything much; she just followed through the channels and did what was necessary to do.

One day, her connection to the divine came to life for her – a life she felt she was beginning to lose. Laying on the couch feeling like the chemo was winning, there was this beautiful warmth of the sun beaming through her living room window. It was the middle of the winter as she lay on the couch praying. She was praying to God and praying to her aunt who had recently passed from cancer.

She was originally planning on doing the cancer walk for her aunt who died. The year was 2005 and she, herself, got diagnosed in October 2005. She was originally going to walk in her aunt's honor, but she then she, herself, got diagnosed.

So she's laying on the couch praying to her aunt and to God, the sun came beaming through the window. All of a sudden, she felt this warmth head to toe as if someone actually laid a blanket on top of her covering her with their light and warmth. She made her declaration, "I'm gonna be okay." She knew in that moment she was going to be okay. Whether it was her aunt coming through or if it was a sign from God or if God sent the Holy Spirit, something stirred inside her soul, telling her she would be just fine. She was going to be okay. This happened to be the only time she was thinking negative, worrisome or fearful thoughts like this chemo is going to do me in and get me. She had this experience and suddenly she knew, she truly was going to be okay.

Afterward, immediately, when she felt this feeling, she felt tears coming down the corner of her eyes.

She trusted the message and, more importantly, the messenger.

She knew cancer wasn't going to get her. She was going to get through this and she was going to be okay.

Her Lesson:

The lesson for her in having breast cancer was in the adoption of this divine attitude from the onset. There was no bitterness not even in the beginning. Her desire is to pass on an important lesson to other women who are experiencing what she experienced.

She was asked by Northshore to do a news conference because she also participated in a clinical trial study. There is a negative association with clinical trial studies. People think there's no hope when they hear the term, clinical trial study. "There's no hope" is not only a myth, but also a misconception. She agreed to the interview, as she was the 7000th participant.

Besides the walk, this news conference was her first experience stepping out of the box. Up close and personal, she, unexpectedly, had to get up on a podium and speak to the people sitting there. Her impression was of being interviewed, but here she was in the position of public speaking.

She had to think quick on her feet and then news 55 quoted her– *"There's always hope, don't give up."* That moment on the couch was the pivotal moment of hope for her. The experience of it all – from her doctor telling her you're going to be okay and able to take care of your family to the overwhelming feeling on the couch – gave her the strength and courage to inform others, *"There's always hope; you're going to do this."*

From the very start she adopted hope as her stepchild. Hope is a very big word – the best four letter word used in the correct manner. There's different ways you can use the word hope. Two more powerful phrases she relies upon are "I will" and "I can," instead of, "I hope I will and I hope I can." This is what got her through.

So feels as though she partnered with the divine in herself, and took on an attitude; an attitude of, "I will" and "I can." There came a feeling that day on the couch of, "it's going to be good." She decided in those moments, she could and she would!

The Blessing:

Her words of wisdom: You are most certainly not in this alone. She wishes someone said this to her because she kept it all inside until it was all over. It wasn't until after her walk when she mustered up the courage to start talking about it.

She asked herself a tough question: What are you doing? So many people wanted to help her, but she didn't allow them to. She wouldn't let them in. She encourages other women to talk, talk, talk about it; there are support groups, breast cancer coalitions, and a whole lot of help out there.

When you reach out to somebody it becomes a contribution to them because they get to be a contribution to you and this makes them feel good.

In the darkest moment of her life, not knowing if she was going to make it, she tapped into God and gave up her fear to trust. She opened up to that connection. This experience, for her, from the beginning was an adaption of a new attitude. She was going to take this on in a way which declared, she may have cancer, but cancer DID NOT have her.

The Inspirational Lesson:

This was her wake up call to realize she needed to start doing things for herself. She basically figured out how to honor herself and to also be a contribution to other people at the same time because of this experience.

Her focus from the onset even in the beginning was how she had a "let's go; it's on" attitude. She recants a memory of running so fast on a treadmill and sending cancer a message; if I have to, I'll out run you.

She took on the spirit of hope. She didn't hold back. There were people who needed to help her so they could feel like the contribution they are. She reminds everyone again; YOU ARE NOT ALONE. People are waiting to embrace you.

She really gave it up when it hit the fan. She let it go and gave it up. She felt the presence of God covering her in a blanket of warmth.

She had the opportunity and the experience to step into not just hoping but BEING hope, as well.

CHAPTER FOUR
HELL NO! I WON'T GO

How did I get here? The hard way.

So, a woman walks into a Catholic church, she got there late, had a fight with her boyfriend on the way and sees her two daughters playing with their hair in a far-off kind of way. Her life was in utter chaos because she chose to attach herself to the wrong man (okay, men – this was her pattern; she did this over and over again). Her underlying subconscious belief she needed to win the love and affection of an emotionally unavailable man in order to validate her drew these very same men toward her.

She began to toy around with spirituality, asking the hard questions, seeking the answers she wanted to hear. At one point, she believes, scripture was being used to manipulate her. Finally, she got fed up! She began to open up the Bible herself (which she had never done before) and read for herself.

She began to visit pastors, connect with other spiritual folks, read different books on various spiritual pathways and even spent hours on search engines for meanings behind scriptures. She uncovered the real meanings (from professionals and scholars) of these Bible phrases; whereas before she felt she might have been manipulated, now she was uncovering the truth. She became a super sleuth of spirituality, but she didn't know who she was in the spiritual world – at least not yet. Was she spiritual or religious? This was the new quest she had to discover or, rather, uncover. There had to be more; *she* had to be more.

Her desperate need for answers as to why she – in her 48 years of life – had never known a healthy relationship with a man. She needed to know why her life was an utter mess from her health and finances to her relationships. Feeling despondent with no answers, she walks into a Christian church and is deeply touched, inspired and moved to tears and she (would never/ever – I mean NEVER put her first foot forward) stands up in front of hundreds of strangers and makes a declaration that her life now belongs to God. "Do with me what you will," she declared.

She extended her hand and said, "Hi, God, I'm Ann." He responded, "I know who you are, but do you know who I am?"

She stepped out of her comfort zone and into the light. She took the first, scariest, bravest and most courageous step of her life. Her soul thrashed about in its quest for more. Little did she know what she had just signed up for. By the way, that woman is me.

Someone told me my life would now be full of turmoil, tests and challenges. I scoffed at the idea. Open up the gates of seething conflict and serendipitous miracles to enter; both at the same time along with passion pain, and lots of praying.

Someone else would come into my life to cause me more pain as my old subconscious ways would continue to insist it was right. That pain was to be my gain now. God used this experience for my highest good (although it certainly didn't feel that way at the time). It would take years of explaining, questioning, and heart wrenching tears, but I never stopped saying, "I don't understand, but I choose faith." Life stuff came my way that would otherwise make anyone else run into the arms of the enemy and sometimes, I did.

I kept getting knocked down but popping back up on my feet like one of those childhood clown toys. No matter how many times you bop them, they pop back up; and God continued to give me a way and a means, although there were many times where I demanded answers as well as solutions and I angrily wanted them now!

Have you ever felt this way? You get really angry at God? You're not alone in feeling this way and you're not alone because God is in you; you haven't realized yet how deeply you are loved and the power you have within. For me there was a battle ensuing; the battle between old and new had begun. Some call it the enemy; I call it the enemy which is my mind.

However, God made it clear, in reality there are two sources - her in partnership with Him.

She would later come to realize how important this one sentence is.

What happens next is the enthusiasm of miracles combined with inner turmoil. Day by day she experiences miracles in her life that can only be from one source. Day by day she experiences conflict within herself, the imposed expectations she placed on herself and those of society. However, God makes it clear, in reality there are two sources; her in partnership with Him, with Him at the realm. She would later come to realize how important this one sentence is.

A single mother (by the way, I coined the phrase "double-mom" it's all a matter of perception), leaving the law firm with no other job to fall back on, no clue as to what she would do, but clearly knowing what she could not do – go another day without being of service to others.

Of course, she did what anybody who believed she had heard the Holy Spirit would do – she said, "Hell no! I'm not good enough."

So be it. Her journey begins. She feels compelled to write for God – even hearing the Holy Spirit guide her to "write in ministry." Feeling this to be her new truth right down to the shivers and shudders her body experienced upon hearing this, her next step is shocking at best. Of course, she did what anybody who believed she had heard the Holy Spirit would do – she said, "Hell no! I'm not good enough." I don't have a degree. I'm not well versed enough in scripture. She was a baby in the world of spirituality and had some soul work to clean up, as well.

Feeling alone and completely abandoned at times, she came to learn that she never truly was alone. God would put people in her path – some of which could be nothing else but angels, some who would hurt her deeply in order to heal her, though He never failed to direct her every footstep – even the stumbling mistakes and the ones that caused her to face-plant in the mud. Big mistakes, at that. It was in the mistakes where she finds the hidden gemstones. He knew the value of her heart. Her head, however, that was another story. God had his work cut out for Him with her. He needed to roll up his sleeves on this one.

We are, fortunately, living in a day and age where transformation and enlightenment are bridging from the exception to the norm. No longer do we have to opt for a mindset that neither serves us nor humanity. We can be open to the possibility that, together partnering with God, we are perfectly capable of creating a reality which is way better than any fantasy.

When we are open to these possibilities, divine creation within us can begin. The signs, the messages, and the possibilities are all there waiting for us to greet them, accept them and embrace them. We can stand up, show up, be a contribution and make a difference. It's all a matter of perception.

CHAPTER FIVE
NO DAY AT THE BEACH:
MY PEACE I GIVE TO YOU;
MY PEACE I LEAVE YOU

No Day at the Beach

Immediately after my entering that Christian church and entering into a newfound faith, I wasn't ready to take off my gloves – my boxing gloves. I had (and to this day still have) a habit of beating myself up. I'm so hard on myself – my own worst critic. "Everybody else" does it right. Do you ever feel this way about yourself?

As it turns out, my youngest daughter was turning 14 and she wanted to have her birthday party at the beach. Not just any beach – the beach where I had fallen for my best friend at a time in my life when I wasn't "supposed to." Although it was in my past, I hadn't learned yet, not only was I forgiven, but I was more than allowed to forgive myself. I didn't get it yet.

Going back there brought up my past. Alone with three children (my youngest at the time was 2 ½) and separated from my husband, I turned to this best friend for comfort and solace; only thing is we fell in love. Although separated, I wasn't divorced yet and felt guilt and shame. We would go to that very same beach for long walks and heartfelt talks. I made a mess out of my life and couldn't possibly bring myself the gift of forgiveness. I was somebody (in my own eyes) who was unforgiveable.

Fast forward to the 14th birthday party. We get to the beach for the day of her party. I'm late as usual (my grandma used to say that I would be late to my own funeral!). I've yet to be on time for much of anything in my life. Guests are arriving and not one single thing is set up from tablecloths to balloons or any food. A mom whom I've never met before asks me if I need help. For once in my martyrdom, I said yes! She turned to me and asked if she could go to her car first and "give" me something.

I was already in turmoil about being there and late. She came back to me and handed me a key chain. The key chain had a bible verse on it which read, *"Peace I leave you, my peace I give you. Not as the world gives do I give to you. Let not your heart be troubled, neither let it be afraid."* Excuse me while I pick my jaw up from the floor. I was blown away.

God used this complete stranger to deliver a message to me - I was forgiven; to forgive myself.

Lesson Learned:

No matter what I do in my present or did in my past, I had the gift of unconditional love and, more importantly, forgiveness. I was allowed to be human. I took the first step, I accepted Christ as my savior and even more importantly entrusted God to partner with me in my life. You too, are loved unconditionally, and forgiveness is a gift for you to open as well. Don't return it unopened. Know that God loves you and create the possibility of trust. Trust in knowing, He loves you enough – no matter what – you are enough! You are perfectly and divinely created; don't doubt God – don't doubt yourself.

After all, if you're created in the likeness and image of God, that's the good news.

Blessing Earned:

I was given a gift that day – the gift of forgiveness, yes, but so much more than that. I was offered the gift of connection and divine communication. Choose to be open and to receive God's holy love and you, too, will receive your very own gifts to open – the gift of connection, communication, and a Christ-centered life, mistakes and all.

When you believe, God will use those lessons and transform them into blessings for your highest good.

CHAPTER SIX
FELICIA'S STORY: THAT AND A QUARTER WILL GET YOU TO THE AIRPORT

Felicia never knew the term "Soul Mate," until she met Frank. She and Frank were planning their future together – a future that would, sadly, never happen. Felicia was being drawn into a whirlwind of romance, happiness and the power and energies of love. Felicia would think of Frank and her phone would ring. She would relish in her soon-to-be new life, her soul bountiful with love, and he would email her. When he was troubled, Felicia could feel Frank's sadness and pain – knowing that all was not well in his world. It was like nothing she had ever experienced before and, even though it did not come to pass, till this day she can still feel his energy. The ties and bonds of love were never severed. However, they had served their purpose and continued on their own paths, each on different avenues.

Felicia and Frank were planning to buy a home together; things were moving swiftly. His case was packed and he was ready to go. He seemed so in love with Felicia, as if love was coming out of his every pore. Frank was supposed to call Felicia; hours passed, days went by and then weeks. She was frantic; none of her calls, texts or messages were returned. He wouldn't take her calls at work. They lived in separate countries, but he would visit the United States monthly to work in his New York City office.

Frank had completely cut her out of his life with no warning and no rhyme or reason. She was sick to her stomach – the not knowing why was strangling and choking her every cell. She had to take action; nothing she was doing was working. She was devastated because she was so in love with him. She couldn't eat, sleep, listen to a song on the radio or watch a movie.

She invented all kinds of things in her head; maybe he was in trouble with the law, maybe he was hurt. She just needed to know.

She didn't know what came over her, but remembered something about putting a coin in your hand and the Holy Spirit and the angels would answer you. Then she took it one step further – she decided to put the coin in her hand and write the words, "Yes" and "No" on a piece of white paper. She was going to ask if Frank still loved her.

The coin would move under her hand and always wind up on the Yes. She even turned the paper upside down, backwards and spun it around. Even flipping it over, the answer was always landing on Yes. This was the only thing that brought her any comfort and gave her the opportunity to have hope and solace, but most of all relief in her heart.

She prayed and she asked the Holy Spirit to guide her. What happens next is nothing short of divine intervention. Felicia would frequently call his New York City office, but no one there ever gave her any information other than he hadn't been in for some time. She needed to find out. She wanted to confront him at his office and talk to him. Felicia had the notion to grab a hold of her calendar and a quarter. She knew that Frank goes to New York City periodically for business. She was desperate for answers, grasping at hope.

She was then inclined to take the quarter and place it on the calendar. With an ever-so-light touch, she was guided to a date on the calendar, June 11th. Over and over again it kept going on to June 11th. She completely believed this was coming from her angels. There was a good feeling of tranquility and peace. She had all but forgotten those feelings the last few weeks, so she felt it was truly divine intervention.

Even though she had used different coins – always a quarter though – Felicia used the same piece of paper. It had all kinds of writings and messages she had written down and she would always try to decode them. And then, June 11th came. Felicia turned to her co-worker to tell her that it was June 11th. Her co-worker was on this journey with her and knew everything. Felicia called Frank's office and lo and behold, he was there. At this point, her heart dropped because he hadn't been to New York the whole time. She had to go see him/confront him. He just HAS to talk to me, she thought through heart-wrenching tears. She was getting angry now along with mixed feelings of anxiousness. She canceled her day at work, was devastated and crying.

Next, she asked her angels to give her a time and also allowed the coin to move freely about as her finger was guided; she was led to 3:00 p.m. on the paper along with other numbers. Together with the date and the time she looked at flights for that particular day. Sure enough, there was a flight leaving to Frank's home town from New York from LaGuardia Airport.

She thought she was insane, but had to follow through – she went to the airport. Felicia took her coin and her paper with her; this is how much she believed. Thoughts of her losing her mind but not being able to stop herself battled for space in her head. The drive seemed like an eternal bad dream where you keep walking in slow motion, never arriving at your destination. Felicia got to the airport, looked up at the board and there it was – the flight number and the time. She began to walk in an excited and hurried way as her breath grew shorter with every step and, there in front of her stood Frank. He was shocked and so was she.

Of course, the first words out of his mouth were, "How did you find me?" Felicia admitted the truth. He was well aware of their connection because he had experienced it too, on many occasions. She felt her chest go numb as she asked him what she needed to know; what she needed to hear. "Why did you do this to me? How could you; we were planning a future together. I need answers. I need closure."

Frank began to explain to her that his reasoning was mostly due in part to his young child and his child's mother. His past was not rectified. There were unresolved issues. He needed to cut all ties with Felicia and do so quickly.

Of course, Felicia had many questions. His answer was always the same – he needed to break all ties with Felicia so that he could move on in peace for both his young child and himself. He told her that he still loved his son's mother. Felicia answered him, "You're lying." She knew better and he didn't deny it either. She could still see in his eyes he had feelings for her.

He also told Felicia, "You love me too much. You know I could never keep you happy." After much conversation, Felicia got the closure she needed, but not the answers she wanted. Her heart hurt for many years and till this day, she could still feel him when he needs her the most. And, true to form, that's when he reaches out for her and contacts her.

Felicia's Lesson Learned:

Felicia's lesson was one of the most painful – when you give your all to someone and attach your hopes, your dreams and your future onto to them and they up and disappear without a word, you give away all of your power. They cut you off as if they cut off your blood supply and oxygen, as well. Felicia went into deep sadness, but the gift waiting on the other side was one she never would have dreamed of either.

Felicia learned that happiness was her responsibility – that it was not someone else's job. She put all of her hopes, dreams and aspirations onto Frank and he felt her vibe. In addition to the possibility of never having a peaceful future because of his baggage, he also realized that he could never live up to that ideal of being responsible for all of her happiness. Most of all, Felicia may have lost someone in her life, but she now had gained a connection with something even bigger!

Felicia's Blessing:

The blessing for Felicia was in that she would now move forward on her path and take responsibility for her own happiness. She came to know freedom both for herself and as a contribution for others. If she took responsibility for her happiness, this could set someone else free.

More importantly, Felicia learned through her painful experience to trust her intuition, to follow the voice of the Holy Spirit. She knew then what she knows now, that in her deepest, darkest and most troubling times, she could turn to God and He would guide her. He would give her the desires of her heart – and, in this instance, it was closure. And, closure is exactly what she got.

Felicia and Frank parted, both knowing each had experienced a love of a higher level – spiritual love. What is spiritual love? Spiritual love is a love which comes not as your greatest and lasting love, but "The One" who teaches you the highest lesson you need to learn so you can move forward in life and in love.

You cannot heal without first having experienced pain.

CHAPTER SEVEN
THE PROVERBIAL WINDS OF CHANGE

Many changes were stirring just as the formation of a hurricane does; as if wind direction were changing while speed was increasing simultaneously in my life. It began with a career change. Leaving the office I worked in for the last, almost-decade which sucked the life out of my soul like a vacuum hungrily ingests its coveted dust was the start. Leaving my job and entering the scary, crazy, fulfilling, why-did-I-do-this world of writing began.

Classes ensued, first creative writing, then grammar, then copy editing, copy writing, and an editorial certificate at a prestigious school. Determined to work from home to care for my ailing parents who lived with me and be there for my three children as a divorced mom, the pursuit of writing opportunities began, as well.

A few years earlier, my parents came to help me because I divorced and I wound up helping them, as well. The true meaning of family, I suppose. You help each other during times of strain, unconditionally. Little did I know that this was part of God's will for my life and His calling upon my life was about to be fulfilled. I had recently reconnected with a girlfriend from high school whose chapter in this book is named, "The Power of Declaration" and she was the one who had reminded me of how my mom came to name me.

Visit me at www.theinspiredlivingnetwork.com to check out all my inspirational and transformational books and services or to contact me for life coaching in spiritual and relationship matters.

I also have a successful caregiver's blog: www.inspirecaregivers.com.

My Transformational Workbook, "Joy-Full Journaling for the Caregiver's Spirit" won the 2016 Fearless Caregiver Award and you can find it here: www.inspirecaregivers.com.

I also have a web writing business that will help you connect and engage with your audience on multiple levels: www.inspirecontent.com.

I've another book being published: Transformational Journaling for Mind, Body, Spirit coming soon, as well as a chapter in a compilation book entitled, "The Peacemakers."

Watch for these at www.theinspiredlivingnetwork.com and on Amazon.com.

My Lesson Learned:

"Trust in the Lord with all Your Heart and Lean not on Your Own Understanding," (NIV Proverbs 3:5.) Sometimes we want to control everything, but it's when we surrender control, that God can move freely in our lives. When we act like bucking broncos, it's hard to get that saddle on and reign us in. It's not that we don't have our own free will, but God can lead us to greener pastures.

My Blessing Earned:

I have a mantra, "I Choose Faith!" I've said this at times with my teeth clenched, but sticking to it in the worst of times has brought me the greatest blessing ever earned. God always sent me an angel, a helper, a shoulder.

CHAPTER EIGHT
POSITIVE PSYCHOLOGY AND THE BIBLE: GOD'S A-NODDING

One of the first writing assignments I had after leaving my office job was working for a positive psychologist writing content for her entire website. One by one, New York Times Best-selling authors and life coaches who made a difference in this world entered my world. Writing their bios was an incredible learning experience.

Fascination and fulfillment took over. Truly wanting to obtain a degree in psychology was a dream that would not be fulfilled for me, as my father began the journey toward the end of his life and needed constant attention in all areas of his life; however, life coaching was an attainable goal I could reach.

Accepting Christ into my life and desiring to become a life coach, resourcefulness set in and I took pride in discovering that I could combine both. I became a Christian Life Coach. One of the Life Coaches on the positive psychologist's website impressed me so much that I just had to subscribe to his writings via my email. Every week I received his newsletter.

Coincidence? I Think Not!

There it was again, that swirling feeling that something good was about to happen, and something great was definitely up. Coincidences began to fly at me as though I were a giant magnet attracting all this into my world. Like-minded people, one by one, appeared into my aura.

Bumping into an old grammar school friend, he suggested that I look into some empowerment seminars he had thoroughly recommended. Here was a spiritually-minded man and, for some reason, I trusted him intrinsically from the moment we reconnected.

Receiving a message that there was an introduction that very evening to those seminars, I made every excuse in the book not to attend; I had an assignment deadline, needed to cook, and my daughter needed a ride somewhere.

The Cowardly Lion

Then the proverbial "it" happened. Something came over me; I ordered a pizza, requested a deadline extension, and got a carpool going for my daughter and off I went. When I arrived at the hotel for the introduction to the seminar, I was frozen paralyzed with fear and immobile in my car in the parking lot; I was too afraid to go in.

Out loud and to myself the questions came flying at me, "What are you doing here? You don't know anyone here. You're here all by yourself – how scary!" A large group of attendees walked behind my car at the moment when I was "debating" with my own self. Figuring that they had seen the crazy lady talking to herself in the car, I mustered up the courage I did not even know existed in my soul.

I walked in, smiling and introduced myself to the first person in my path. One of the "assignments" for the evening was to get up and walk across the room and introduce yourself to a stranger. Upon returning to my seat, there was a woman sitting there.

Feeling awkward and uncomfortable, I clumsily reached under the seat and secretly tried grasping for my pocketbook so I could make a graceful exit. She saw me, I was busted. She wound up speaking with me the entire night about her experience in taking the forum and I signed up right there on the spot.

This was a game-changer and a life-changer for me. Not only did it change my world, I made friends for life. This woman was another like-minded individual that came into my universe.

Serendipity Begins

One month after taking this forum, I received a newsletter from the Life Coach I mentioned earlier; it stated he was one of the original creators of this forum!

Blown away doesn't even begin to describe the feeling that knocked me in my gut. Here I was writing content for this man, not knowing that he was one of the original contributors to this wonderful forum, bumping into a friend I had not seen nor heard from in over 30 years – that's right 30 years - who recommended this forum to me.

Divine Serendipity had only just begun.

My grammar school friend, in the meantime, had added me to a mailing list for one of his favorite bloggers. "Coincidentally" enough, my first published piece was on a spiritual writer's association where she was featured.

Coincidences…I think not.

The Lesson:

Be open to the notion there is something higher than you or your ego. Be open to the thought process of a divine source whose name is God is available to you, lives in you and is willing to show you the way.

The Blessing:

All you have to do is follow along the journey, be open to receive the secret clues and the not-so-subtle messages. Run, play, flow and enjoy the journey. Open up to spirit and open up your own spirit.

CHAPTER NINE
THERESA TELLS HER TALE:
ALL MOTHERS ARE HOLY

What's in a Name?

Theresa was in her glory; she was pregnant again. It was her fifth pregnancy of which she only bore three children. She miscarried a set of twin baby girls on her fourth pregnancy. She had given birth to three boys already and was beyond certain she would have another boy.

One evening as she and her husband lay in bed, upon looking through baby books for boys' names, she turned to her husband to ask his opinion, but he was already on his way to sleepy land. Men! She thought to herself and went back to the business at hand. She had already had three sons; John, Thomas, and Robert and was considering Steven or Michael as a baby name.

Theresa's husband did not care much either one way or the other. He had a mantra for a happy marriage – always saying that it all boiled down to two words, "Yes, dear!" Theresa kept looking at the book and felt sleepy. She turned to her husband and said, "to be continued." She put the lights out and went to sleep to her husband's delight. She fell asleep and woke up in the middle of the night. She didn't know what time it was and felt as though she were in a daze.

She was half asleep and half awake and quite restless. She usually slept on her left side because she was deaf in her left ear.

She made herself comfortable and positioned herself to fall back to sleep on her left side so her right ear could be in tune with listening for the other children. She turned around and faced the window, trying to get even more comfortable without much success.

Upon taking her hand out from underneath the blanket and resting it on top of the blanket, Theresa felt something restless about these following moments. She wasn't awake, but not quite asleep either. She felt as though she were in twilight – the time before sunset, but when it is still a bit dark outside. Trying once again to get in a comfortable position – as comfortable as she could be - being five to six months pregnant – she picked her hand up to put it back under the blanket. Her hand seemed to have a mind of its own and did not want to cooperate, so she left it out again. Although hard to explain, Theresa did not know what to do with her hand – it seemed to be the most restless limb of her body at this point.

With her left hand on the left side of her face and her right hand in the open palm position, is where she saw the vision. The vision was of the Blessed Mother, Mary, mother of Jesus. She was kneeling beside Theresa's bedside and she put her hand on top of Theresa's, not holding it or grasping it, only laying it on top. And then she spoke.

"Name your baby girl, Ann Elizabeth." And then she was gone. That was it. Theresa remembered she had her knees up close to her body, as much as could accommodate being pregnant when she had this vision and from that position, she straightened out and she sat up in bed. Theresa thought to herself what a weird dream; however, going back to sleep was impossible as it did not seem like a dream at all, but more of a vision.

Till this day, Theresa describes this vision as that of being in a trance, not fully awake, but not sleeping either. It was hypnotic for her. Theresa did not know if it was a dream or if it was reality. As she was laying there trying to fall back to sleep, she kept looking back down at her hand as if to say, "Did she really touch me? Was it really real?" She lay there all night trying to make sense out of it, to see if it was real. It seemed so vivid, it couldn't have been a dream nor her imagination.

Theresa is 91 as she recants this story, which she has done on many occasions. As she looks into the far off past and remembers, you can tell she still sees and believes in her heart this did occur for her. She remembers it all in vivid detail. Not bad for a 91-year-old woman.

She told her husband the next day and his response was, "It was probably a dream." Theresa believingly told him, "I guess we're going to have a girl and we should name her Ann Elizabeth." Theresa's husband skeptically questioned her and asked, "So, you're going by this dream and where did you come up with a name like that?"

Theresa never thought about another baby girl's name, feeling if she did have a girl, that was it – her name would be Ann Elizabeth.

However, when she told her mother who was a steadfast woman of faith who prayed the rosary daily and lived to the splendid age of 99, her reply matched that of a woman of true faith. "Wait, and see what happens. If it's a girl, you name her Ann Elizabeth and listen to the vision."

For many nights after that, she would go to sleep and wonder if she would have the same dream and if it would happen again. She never looked at names after that. She made up her mind if it was a girl it would be Ann Elizabeth and if it was a boy, she would address it then.

A few months later, Theresa went into labor. She had a long and arduous labor, surprisingly for her fourth child birth. And lo and behold, to Theresa's delight and surprise, she had indeed given birth to a baby girl, whom of course she named Ann Elizabeth.

Today, Theresa comments that it's funny because none of her other children had middle names given to them.

Theresa's Lesson:

Theresa was always a devote believer and a woman of faith, just like her mother. During those last few months of her pregnancy, with no sonograms back then to offer proof either one way or another, Theresa learned to stop asking why when it came to the sudden miscarriages of her twin baby girls at six months pregnant and to trust and wait on the Lord for a new blessing – a named baby girl called Ann Elizabeth. Theresa had to learn patience, perseverance and the highest of faith. She had to wait to see if this were the truth, a dream or a vision or, perhaps a little bit of all three.

Theresa's Blessing:

Theresa's blessing came in the form of a baby girl after having three sons and miscarrying two twin girls. Theresa's blessing also came in the form of what would be her future caregiver. Ann Elizabeth became caregiver to both her father and her mother. Funny thing, though, they moved in to help her through her divorce and she wound up becoming caregiver to them both. There is a saying that caregivers are chosen by God – perhaps this was the blessing that was meant to be after all. By the way, that baby girl – she's me. My name is Ann Elizabeth and if I could only hope and wish to live up to it in any way, shape or form, I'd be humbled tenfold.

The meanings behind the names Ann and Elizabeth are God's favor and grace.

CHAPTER TEN
"THINK" GOD AND CARRY A BIG STICK

With a background of foster homes and runaway centers, and as difficult a childhood as you could ever imagine but wouldn't want to, a young boy could go in any direction, but this young man made a choice. He chose to be spiritual and to talk to God. In the worst of situations, what had pulled him out of depression and keeping him from anger was God. The presence of God was always there for him without much mentorship or practical experience, God was inside this young boy. The actual hardships in his life were the very things that brought him closer to God.

Most people in the worst of times (self included) get angry at God sometimes; ask why, blame God, but not this young man.

His trials became his testimony and he became closer to God.

He believes that God protected him from a lot of hardships. What an amazing statement for someone who had a really hard life. Instead of turning away from God, he turned toward God. He feels that God turned toward him and pulled him out of some really tough stuff. It was like God chose him because he wasn't really searching for God, but God found him anyway. He didn't know much of how to pray, but he had a spiritual connection regardless.

When he was six or seven years old, he was abandoned by his mom and he was sent to his grandmother, who was abusive. He found himself homeless, sometimes in the middle of the winter on top of rooftops with no place to sleep. In the middle of snow in the city, sitting there hanging from the ledge thinking about committing suicide he would hear God say to get back up. He began to meditate sitting there without even knowing what meditation was. He was all of seven years old. That's when he knew God had intentions for him and he understood a little bit more about spirituality.

He remembers a foggy memory at maybe four or five years old too; he was a devilish little kid, he says with a grin, a daredevil. He would go and explore. One time he was at a canal and he was looking down from a bridge, and he fell. He remembers some other force picking him up and putting him back on the bridge. He never hit the water, but a supernatural force brought him back to the bridge. He felt something lifting him up and putting him on top of this bridge. He was a little kid and he didn't know much about it at the time. As he got older though, he looks back and is astonished at having had this experience. It still remains a distant, foggy recollection, but a memory still the same. After all, how could you forget something like that?

He had this presence of God with him ever since he was a little child. He also recalls a time when he would go visit an extended relative and, even as a child, he could feel negativity, supernaturally in the house. His positive spirit and upbeat attitude was always in conflict with the negativity he felt there. He would sleep as much as he could until it was time to leave.

Fast-forward to him in his early twenties, having met a pretty cool roommate – a female – who deepened his practice of faith and spirituality. One night, they were sitting on top of their mattresses and both of them were out of work. There was no food and no money; they were pretty hungry. They were sipping water and pretending it was a juicy, steak. This got them through the night, but when morning came they were starving. They were living in Miami and, with nothing much else going on, chose to head down to the beach and that's when he saw a big stick.

In letters as big and bold as you can imagine, about three feet according to his recollection, he began to write the letters, **"THINK GOD,"** right then and there in the sand. Not "thank God," but "think God." They both were writing this in the sand.

They began to walk further along down the beach and the next thing they knew they ran into a company picnic, and some guy yelled out to them. "Hey, do you guys want something to eat? Come over here and put on these bracelets." With those bracelets, they were able to eat all day, drink some beer, and they even got to take some food home with them. This all happened immediately after they had written, *"Think God,"* in the sand.

Their reaction was that this was pretty incredible as they sat there looking at the ribs and corn they had brought home. Things like this just kind of flowed for him throughout his life, but this was pretty spectacular.

The next set of questions I had for him was how he had this "flow" in his life for these incredible happenings, how does he allow God into his life, and how has he connected with God since childhood, and he answers that he just allows God in his life. Sometimes people go to church, they pray, they talk to Him or they praise Him, but the way that he connects with God is inspiring.

The way he connects with God is simply beautiful – he connects with God by giving!

According to him, this is how he connects with the Divine: "The more I give, the more I connect with God and that's how I say thank you to Him. The way I think about giving is like a majestic lion, and he looks beautiful and you want to hug him because he has that big mane and all, but what stops you from giving him food, from wanting to protect his environment, and to help him? You get eaten! This is the same way I feel when I help people; it's possible they are going to step all over you or take advantage of you, and push everything they could in your face. Why should that change me? I don't let other people stop me from being who I am. I go ahead and help them anyhow. I don't let that stop me."

"I don't let how other people react change how I act."

Sometimes I feel guilty because it's actually a selfish feeling because it feels so good to give. The way that you thank God is by giving. And it does work for me because I don't take anything personally.

He tells his kids all the time, when you are born God gives you a paper bag, and you put your blessings in that paper bag. So, you have to start giving in order to receive new blessings. I tell them all the time, when you were 2 years old, that Barney costume was your biggest blessing and now you're 14-years-old and you have an Xbox. So, now you have to give that Barney costume away to somebody else, figuratively speaking.

We have a certain amount of time in this world and only so much that we need. So, by giving it away, it's kind of like a blessing boomerang; it comes back to you in a good way.

This shows strength of character, a person who knows who he is and that he is a person who likes to give. He just continues to give unconditionally. He can be who he is, stay in that place and stay in that space no matter how somebody else receives or reacts. He gives unconditionally, and it just works for him. It's so unconditional, it's mind-blowing; it reminds me of how God loves us.

So, there he is at the beach saying, **"Think God,"** they smack into a company picnic, get a belly full of food, food to take home, (and beer/don't forget the beer!), and life is good. What an amazing outlook on life. What a perfect role model of unconditional giving and an example to share this with his kids; he can tell these stories to his kids because they are a captive audience. With older people, he can just show it by being who he is as a role model.

The Lesson:

You can turn toward God in the deepest and darkest times or you can turn away. You have a choice.

To him, it doesn't matter what other people think, say and do, he is who he is, he's going to give unconditionally, bottom line. Emotions are not situations; a person can be devastated by something huge or small. We get to choose at any given moment, it's okay to feel, but it's also okay to choose how you're going to feel something, for how long, and how you are going to recreate it. The most important thing is to be honest with yourself. Don't stay in any one emotion for too long. You can be angry because that anger can tell you that something is not working in your life, and then you can turn anger into action. Then you can take responsibility and you don't have to stay in an angry mood. God intends for us to be successful; it's our birthright; God intends for us to be the most we can be.

The Blessing:

The blessing here is in staying in his integrity, not only is he a contribution to others, but the blessings boomerang has no choice but to find him. It's people like him, being upbeat, being energetic, giving unconditionally; he's a contribution to the world giving unconditionally. Whether you are someone who talks in front of thousands of people or you are just someone who smiles at everyone you meet, you are both an equally massive contribution. Sometimes you think you have to reach millions and ask "what is my purpose, or I have to do this great thing." What you are doing as a human being and being yourself is the same thing as being a millionaire or talking in front of thousands of people. It doesn't always have to be this great big thing we think it is. His being faithful writing "Think God" led him right to the barbeque buffet. He gave it up to God; he was at the closest place he could be to connect with God at the beach. And there was God saying I'm going to take care of your needs.

Being at the right God place at the right God time, he had a God Nod!

CHAPTER ELEVEN
(THIS WAS AN ABSOLUTE COINCIDENCE/I KID YOU NOT!) IT'S 11:11 AND ALL IS WELL

If you're like me and you are reading this book, chances are you have seen the number 1111 or 111 in some way, shape or form. Wherever I went, I began to see the numbers 1111 or even 111.

Those numbers followed me around during the day when I glanced at the clock, when I turned the radio on and the announcer announced it's 11:11, and even cars that pulled in front of me with license plate number 1111. To much of this, I say thankfully, I have witnesses.

One evening on the way to a birthday party wherein a request for "no gifts" was made, I stopped into the card store with my cousin. My cousin was out of my life for so long, but as all this began, she reappeared. She is a woman of faith if there ever was one. We wanted to purchase a picture frame and simply put a card inside. She handed me a card and said how about this one? The card had the Bible verse on the front of it (Hebrews 11:1) about faith is believing in things unseen.

I never told her yet about seeing the numbers 111 or 111 for fear of her thinking I was nuts, but that night I shared with her.

Another time, my girlfriend from high school and I were chatting away one evening and both said goodnight only to text each other at the same time asking if the other noticed that our phone call ended at 11:11. We giggled like we were back in high school again. She is one of my highest spiritual friends.

Once again, on another occasion, upon meeting a new friend on social media, we said good night at the same time. She "Laughed Out Loud" and said that our conversation ended at 11:11. I just met her! How could she know anything about that? She said it was her belief that those numbers were little winks from angels. I had never heard this before.

Hebrews 11:1 is my favorite verse; so much so that my college daughter bought me a giant wall inscription with the verse on it. I take that verse everywhere with me and whenever I see those numbers I say out loud, "I CHOOSE FAITH!"

Just last week, I was so sad and disappointed. I experienced the loss of my mother recently, my daughter going into college and someone I care deeply for was relocating. It was all too much, too soon. I found three pennies on the floor while at the mechanics and I looked at my car's clock and it was 1:11. My angels were smiling at me and letting me know it was all going to be just fine.

All I had to do was be sure of what I hope for and certain of blessings unseen.

"Now faith is confidence in what we hope for and assurance about what we do not see." Hebrews 11:1 (NIV)

CHAPTER TWELVE
ARE _YOU_ MY SOUL MATE?
WHAT'S IN A NAME?

I have an intention for the title of one of my future books to be, "Are YOU My Soul Mate? Relationships, Reflections, and Revelations." There's a whole book in there to delve into this touching and heartwarming subject.

As I went along my journey, coincidences and serendipities swirled around me like the tornado in the Wizard of Oz. Sometimes, I too, found myself in strange places wishing to "go home again." I so wanted to hold onto the old, familiar yet limiting and self-sabotaging beliefs that were so ingrained in me. Letting go and recognizing that I had the power within the whole time required a sort of bravery I was not yet ready for, and wouldn't be for a long time. I had to first follow the yellow brick road, face my lions, tigers, and bears and meet the wicked witch – oh yes, I did! I was determined, however, to meet the wizard.

God knows I am a fiercely determined woman (okay, okay, somewhat stubborn); God sent the best of the best my way to break me in order to make me. I took on the assignment and I'd like to say I got an A for effort; but, really in the end it's not the grade – it's the fact you held on to the end, rode the wave and wound up somehow miraculously standing on your own two feet feeling more like your "self" than ever before, but you can't ride the wave until you dive into the ocean.

Hi, my name is Ann and I had a repetitive pattern of attracting relationships with men that wouldn't work for me. The old me would say "they were narcissists," but the new me can be vulnerable and raw, telling you the truth. I was a co-dependent. You see, they could not have showed up as narcissistic if I wasn't "being" co-dependent.

If you've ever had the experience of being a co-dependent, you know what I'm referring to. My experience from childhood was a story in my mind that went a little something like this: "Emotional coldness, distance, and love came from the same people and both were so intertwined, I didn't have the capability to notice the difference. Love and harsh experiences were one and the same."

Add to that the fact that I was (and still am) an empath. I feel everybody's stuff; and live fully and deeply into this thing called life. Joy is ecstasy, sadness is devastating. As the new and grown-up version of me, I've learned to use what I like to call, "my compassion dial." There are times to feel sorrow and sadness and times to walk away from toxic behavior. I don't have to stay. I get to choose. Choosing is hard sometimes, though, isn't it? You can choose powerfully, however.

All of the "should haves," the red flags and the signs were there, but I didn't have the skills – even as an adult I sheepishly admit, I still falter at times, but am happy to report getting better – to put up clear boundaries. I loved with all I had; I trusted with all I had; I gave it all away. And then, I began to do the work. I read, prayed, researched, talked, dug and dug even deeper – you would think I'd have reached China by now with how deep I dug to discover or rather uncover the multiple layers of my "self." Here are a couple of things I learned along my painful journey; If I can help you save some time, some anguish or gain a little glimmer of insight and clarity, it would make my heart sing:

Unconditional Love

Along my journey, I met someone who could either take me down the rabbit hole or make me stand up and fight – kicking down doors in high heels of course! I chose both. I ran from him and returned to him, rinse, repeat, rinse and repeat again. He was truly my soul mate; not in the romance novel type of soul mate, but "the one" who came down here from heaven to teach me the lessons I REFUSED to learn. That's right; it was not until I was willing to take responsibility for my life (I was THE LAST person on earth you could have told to take responsibility – ewwww!), that my life truly became "My Life!"

You see the secret about unconditional love is one thing and one thing only; you accept the other wholeheartedly, but you keep your boundaries in place. Talk about a balancing act! When you are in relationship with another being, it's never really all about you; it's about them and their silly human stuff too. You see, they have their own stories too; you are simply playing a part for them, as you play your own role.

Of course, I knew the term "soul mate." Who didn't? However, a big however, I had never heard the term "Twin Flame" until my soul sister enlightened me. I was convinced this man was my "Twin Flame," but I like to coin the term "Spirit Mate."

I would think of him; my phone would vibrate; it was him. I would feel his energy and would say his name out loud and there would be an email that wasn't there a few minutes ago.

Everywhere I went – I truly mean just about everywhere – his name would show up (and he does not have a common name at all), a conversation he and I just had, would show up in the form of an email or social media post, and I would feel him so deeply like nothing I ever knew or could even begin to put into translatable words. I instinctively knew when he was thinking of me or ready to send me a message of some sort. We took photos together and in those photos, there were orbs that would show up.

One day, I had to take my poor sick pup to the veterinarian's. They took him from me to care for him and I went over to the sink to wash my hands; and, there next to the sink, was a doggie bone jar in the shape of a doggie and on his name tag was my friend's name with a cute little slogan on it. I laughed with all my heart.

On another occasion, I broke down and cried. While out to lunch in a faraway place with a new female friend I'd met at a mastermind group, the waitress took our information down and then asked the gentleman next to me what his name was. Of course, it was the same name as my friend's. There were songs with his name on it, writing assignments came my way with nicknames that had his name in them, even signs on streets. This happened for years, but this time, at the restaurant I broke down and cried.

I called him; I couldn't take it anymore. "What do you want with me? Who are you? Who sent you?" His response was classic: "It's just me honey, with you all the time." When my dad was passing, I went up to the hospital and asked if the priest had been up to see my dad to give him last rights; the answer was, of course, that the priest who gave my dad last rights had the same name as my friend.

I choose to believe that my dad was setting things up for someone to watch out for me and to teach me the lessons I needed to learn about valuing and loving myself, as dad began to leave this earthly realm. It was his last dying gift to me; somehow maybe it was his way of saying all he could not say to me when he was alive. I needed to learn to love, honor, and value myself; this was my biggest life lesson. I learned my value and worth do not come from anyone else or anything else – not a lover, a friend, a degree or any amount of accolades or finances. It came from me; period.

Excuse me for a minute while I get a tissue; talk about unconditional love. Dad loved me so much he orchestrated someone to make me cry, make me learn, make my heart sing, soar, sink, and dance all at the same time. As of this writing, I learned something else – and I want this for you too.

Whenever I go into "wounded little girl" mode, I ask myself an important question, "What would powerful woman Ann do in this moment?" She would love herself exactly as she loves her own children – unconditionally, without thinking and without blinking; just effortlessly and gracefully with ease and flow. And my life becomes transformed; it becomes transparent, and it becomes mine!

With him, I learned how to unlock the secrets of independence as I shed the skin of dependency like a snake. I stepped into the shoes of the woman I was meant to be when I allowed the little girl inside of me to take a nap.

And, when she comes out to play and have her way, I love her unconditionally too with all I have. She's my responsibility and no one else's. As long as I stay in this space and in this place, life works for me. Some days my inner little girl is unruly, stubborn and willful and I allow her to have her tantrum and throw herself on the floor exasperated until she is spent. Nothing left to talk about, think about or try to figure out. She goes to sleep and wakes up feeling refreshed and renewed; until next time she comes out to play.

Sometimes I coddle and nurture her and other times I let her have her way until she wears herself out. Sometimes I try to teach her how to comfort herself and other times she teaches me about unconditional love more than anyone else I know.

Without my soul mate, I wouldn't have learned to navigate these tricky waters. He challenged me, dared me and exasperated me. The more he threw my way, the more determined I became to catch it and recreate whatever it was he delivered, and mold it into something which would work. Many times I succeeded and blew him away; other times I backslid.

I thought, I talked, I wrote, but mostly I grew and I transformed. He still comes to me in my dreams up until recently telling me things such as, "The situation in your life right now – you know you are the one creating it," or something like, "Annie, choose faith over fear. You always get to choose."

Tears well up in my eyes as I remember the memories of him; the power, the pain, the lessons and the blessings. I wouldn't change a damn thing. I consider myself truly blessed to be able to say I met my spirit mate here on earth. More importantly, he sacrificed his life here on earth for me, so I could transform, grow, and go on to help others. Maybe, just maybe, he has his own little boy inside, and every so often he'd let down his walls, drop his own mask. In those moments, far and few between, sparse and fleeting, our spirits did recognize each other with an unspoken, "Oh, there you are! I recognize you and I found you once again."

The Lesson:

It's no one else's job to validate you. Your ego strives to make or get that one person who doesn't quite love you the way you need to be loved, to love you better and more than anyone else. It's a missing piece of the childhood puzzle which may still be unresolved. Only difference is, you can resolve it on your own.

You get let go of trying to "win" unavailable love and affection from a man in order to be validated.

You absolutely can create a new story of already being loved and adored in your own right just by being you.

You can allow the right man to win/gain your love and affection instead of you working so damn hard to win it for yourself.

Let go of winning; don't chase/try to win/hold onto unavailable love.

There's an old saying in the world of breakups: "It's not you, it's me." Well, in these cases – it could very well be them and not you.

> *Sometimes others are unavailable for their own reasons, and it's not you who is unlovable; and don't you ever forget it! Hugs!*

The Blessing:

Once you learn to take back your power and take responsibility for validating yourself, two things happen: One is becoming empowered in your own journey and validating yourself in your own right and the other is being a contribution to another.

Nobody wants the job of constantly having to validate another human being. It's too much work. In creating the possibility of validating yourself you set yourself free and, equally as important, you set another human being free. The possibility of freedom is exhilarating for all.

CHAPTER THIRTEEN
A LITTLE BIT OF HEAVEN GOES A LONG WAY
ISN'T THERE SOMETHING MORE THAN THIS?

If you're like most people, you've asked this question: "Isn't there something more than this?" For Samantha, not only was she going to ask the hard questions, she was going to get the hard answers too.

Samantha's inquiry about the difference between religion and relationship brought forth the most amazing creation.

One day Samantha happened to be driving. She saw a cross on top of a church, and she remembers actually saying out loud, "What is it about the name Jesus that is so powerful? Why does it cause some people to love and some people to hate; some people to die for it and some people to kill for it; what is the power of the name Jesus that is unlike any other God name that makes people universally respond in such extremes one way or the other in good or in bad; what's the power in that name???"

Samantha's search began.

Like most of us, Samantha had questions and she was searching for that "something more" we all seek. Samantha is an inspiration in that she was open to asking the hard questions and she got the answers that she never would have expected.

She found that elusive "something more," not only for herself but in ministry and contribution for others in a global - yes, global - way.

Samantha knew she was searching and she just KNEW there was more. She didn't want to go to a rabbi because she felt that he would only want to lead her to Judaism. She was already there; she didn't want to go to a priest because she was worried he would lead her into Catholicism. Samantha just wanted to go to someone who could tell her who the Messiah was. So, she ended up asking an employee of hers who always had their Bible with them.

However, instead of that person gently sharing with her through the scriptures, the truth and the possibility that it could even be Jesus, instead this person started screaming and yelling at her "say this prayer, say this prayer." Samantha was so taken aback.

What she didn't know back then was the prayer she was yelling at her to say was the sinners' prayer. From Samantha's perspective as a Jewish woman, it brought such fear upon her in that moment. She made meaning out of it that God was punishing her for daring to look elsewhere. Such was not the case. What happens next is the biggest blessing not only for Samantha but for the hundreds of thousands she would reach globally through a new ministry. God was going to use her to create something bigger than she could have ever imagined.

God was about to use her worst of circumstances and turn them into the best of times.

All Samantha could think at this point was how His word says, "There shall be no other God but me." She continued questioning and searching. And it was there in that space, that God met her full on. Imagine how delighted He must have been that she was asking questions and seeking answers. Picture this to be the biggest delight God could ever hope for; in the space where people seek Him out, and He gets to meet them full on. Samantha wondered if the Messiah had already come? What if, instead of me waiting for the Messiah, he already came, was the burning question in her soul and in her spirit.

Unfortunately, Samantha would be delayed by the biggest enemy there is – the delay each one of us know personally by name – the enemy called fear. In that moment, she found herself saying the prayer to this employee just so she would leave. Samantha began saying to God, "I'm so sorry, I'll never question again." She was so shook up, do you know what happened next? She began to open up to the possible inquiry of "What if God showed up as love instead of fear?" The undercurrent of courage was beginning to swirl.

Fear, however, delayed her search for the Messiah and she went full fledge into New Age at the same time she also began the journey to opening up to love over fear. Samantha recognized in herself that everything she did in her relationship with God was based on fear of Him. Going to temple was based on not wanting to be left out of the lamb's book of life. She went out of fear not out of love.

How powerful is that for someone to admit? Have you ever taken on a relationship with God with a fear-based mindset? Many people do, only to miss out on the greatest love there is – unconditional love.

In my interview with Samantha, I asked her the following question: "What made you go from Judaism to New Age to where you are at now? What was the Bridge?"

Her answer delighted me: "The bridge was love," she answered.

At the worst part of her life, with no money and nowhere to live, two of the gentlest people she had ever met came back into her life. A while before, she had gone to see an apartment this couple had. It didn't work out; however, fast forward to Samantha finding out she now had to leave her current apartment immediately. With very little money and questioning God, "Why would you do this to me?" her phone rings. It's that sweet, gentle couple from the past (coincidentally) leaving a message on her phone, telling her they remembered her from the past and the apartment is vacant once again, would she be interested. God was nodding.

Unfortunately, Samantha had to do one of the hardest things in her life; she had to tell them she was interested but didn't have enough money. They told Samantha they had prayed on it, and they took her in anyway. Could you imagine how led this couple was by the Holy Spirit to do such a thing – especially in today's world? And there was Samantha's bridge of love. All she had to do was walk across. This couple were Christians and they loved Samantha as Christ loved us. Here's the key for Samantha. They never preached Jesus to her – they **were** Jesus to her; they modeled and represented him like no other. Samantha says they loved her into the kingdom. They even fed her when she had no money for food.

To her shock, Samantha didn't have to wonder much longer why God was having her move; there was a fire in the house she was being forced to move out of a mere few days after she left there. God was not only nodding; He was orchestrating His divine plan for her very life.

So, now Samantha had one of her answers to the question that we all ask God, "Why, God, why?" but that's not even the best part of Samantha's tale of divine serendipity. It gets mightier. Hold onto your seats now.

This couple was, for Samantha, love in action. They were kind and gentle but oh so powerful in their kindness. Samantha went on to become a believer and to also honor the beliefs and faiths of all other people on the same basis – the basis of love; sweet, beautiful, delightful, unconditional love. Here's the best part and the real meaning behind Samantha's story.

The wife had asked Samantha to help host her husband's birthday party because she was so shy, and didn't feel she could do it alone. Samantha was more than willing to oblige. Jokingly, she added, that as long as she didn't have to cook, it was all good. On a more humorous note, Samantha didn't realize that the gentlemen sitting next to her the whole time at that same party, who was wearing an Izod shirt, was actually the reverend from the couple's church. She half-jokingly asked him (as she back-tracked her entire conversation with him in her mind's eye), "Did I curse at all during the time I sat next to you?" He just laughed. Because of the warmth and love she felt that day at the party, she went to church for the first time in her life. There were hundreds of people there, but to this day, Samantha is convinced that the message of the day was just for her.

Samantha invited her parents one day to join her in church; and they did. Samantha wanted to have her experience be about relationship with God and not about religion. It had to show up, for her, as a spiritual experience and not a religious one. And, that's when it happened.

There was a call for volunteers for mission work. Samantha could not sit in her seat. Torn between what God's will for her was and her parents Jewish background and faith, Samantha was overcome with thoughts and emotions. She asked the Holy Spirit, what do I do? Again, she received an answer, "What would you do if your parents weren't here in this moment?" Samantha got up and walked down the aisle and stood up in front of everyone declaring she would go into mission work as she heard her mother cry out, "My baby, my baby." That's when it happened.

Samantha asked God, "Isn't there somewhere right here in Long Island where our own people are hurting instead of going to Africa, where you could use me?" This was the beginning of the creation known today as "Samantha's Li'l Bit of Heaven."

Shortly after this, she was watching television one day and saw a horrible tragedy where a young girl from Long Island had been kidnapped. Samantha could not wrap her head around this; she prayed so fervently for this girl and they came forward to say that they found her.

Samantha could not get past that someone who knew this girl, who was her neighbor, had done this to her. They could have been her hero and instead became her predator and she was sobbing and grieving to the core for this girl. Samantha could not get past this kind of evil and cried out to God, "I don't get this world, I don't understand it, I hate it, and I don't want to be a part of it." Samantha asked out loud, "God, can't there be a place for good people?" Again, God answered her questions, Samantha clearly and audibly heard two words: "That's Heaven."

Samantha wasn't done with her questions for God, she challenged her inquiry further: "God, can't there be a little bit of heaven here on earth where the good people can go?"

At this point, I had to tell Samantha that my chills had chills and asked her what she did next.

Samantha began to write her vision down based on Habakkuk 2:3-4

"And the Lord says, write your vision down plain on tablets and although it may tarry, in His appointed time, He will bring it to pass."

She began to write her vision down on paper. If there was a little bit of heaven on earth, what kind of place would it be?

Come one Come all

If there was a place, it would look like a haven, a refuge, an oasis, a place away from our trials, away from our issues. It would have to be for all ages – it had to be just like the real heaven; it would be for everyone who enters.

(Over the 20 years since it was opened Samantha's Li'l bit of Heaven has seen the youngest guest in the womb and the oldest was 110 years young!).

We are all the Same: Love Knows no Differences

A place open to all so that we could begin to celebrate differences and stop being so divided by them. That's why we have the cross with the Jewish star on it, says Samantha. Can't we celebrate instead of being divided?

There has to be Chocolate!

Chocolate! If it was going to be heaven on earth, it would have to have chocolate! So she devised an idea about serving coffee and cake.

Let the Music Drift You Away

She felt it needed to have music because it's so healing; but with all different tastes, so we have Motown to Latin and Jazz and the common thread would be the message in the music and every song would have a message of hope which would inspire and encourage.

A line in a song can totally change a person's life; it could be an answer to a prayer and they hear it in a song because they are captivated by the music. Then it happens, everything shuts down and there's no preaching, but open hearts ready to receive the message within the music. Music became the universal language.

A Whole Lotta Class

Next thought was classes, workshops, support groups, Bible studies. Nobody was really looking how God's word could truly set you free; it was important to facilitate bereavement or divorce support groups and classes with anxiety, depression, and fear where they were bringing forth in the faith. It wasn't going to simply be, "Just have faith" or "Here's a pill," but rather, how can we use God's word to obtain victory spoken into our lives.

This was 20 years ago, so it was very new to think of declaring and using "It is written" for each and every situation. Samantha wanted people to live a more victorious life. It was going to be one place that was so loving, it was like "a little bit of heaven here on earth." Samantha took what her landlords did for her and gave it an atmosphere, like multiplying it, and giving birth to it at the same time.

Samantha took what her landlord did for her and gave it away; she didn't hold on to it. "Samantha's Li'l bit of Heaven" was born.

Samantha shared her vision with her girlfriend who asked a natural question, "So, when are you going to do this?" Samantha defiantly answered, "I'm **not** going to do this; I have no money and I have no clue or know how to open or run this, I don't even know how to make coffee either; I can't."

Her girlfriend replied, "Wow, this sounds like God to me because when you can't, God can. I want to challenge you to bring this list to a prayer group and get together with a powerful group of people in their prayer walk, and let's pray over this list, and if God wants it to happen, He'll bring it to pass."

Within weeks, every single thing on the list was provided supernaturally. No one ever gave her money, she consistently tells people to encourage them, "Sometimes God does not provide the finances, He provides the favor."

Wherever they looked, there was something on their list. On a Sunday night at the end of a garage sale, they found something on the list; a restaurant was closing and had all the furniture you see at A Li'l bit of Heaven out on their front lawn. Samantha asked if she could have it, and the response was something like, "Sure if you can haul it you can have it."

On April 8, 1994, a teeny, tiny place came to be the original Li'l bit of Heaven. The awning hanging over the coffee counter inside the new location is the original awning from the first place. That's there for Samantha to remember that this place really belongs to the Lord because what God does, He can expand. That awning has been there for more than 20 years.

It was created with no money; it's a labor of love, no pay, just volunteers and the favor of God upon them. Additionally, there were many endless ministries birthed through here where people came here supernaturally and their dreams and life purposes were born. When you use your gifts, it's a joy and not a chore.

The representation of Samantha's Li'l bit of Heaven is identical of what you would imagine heaven to be; a place that is giving beautiful souls this soft incubator to nurture and grow without anyone saying, "You can't or you're not good enough." You have your own cheerleading squad – like your own personal angel team – encouraging you.

And it's in that space of courageously claiming your opportunity, where you know the moment you step into your destiny, there's no turning back. You know you can't do anything else.

"Samantha's Li'l bit of Heaven is so much more than a coffee house or a business. It's a vision. It's a place where you can have a personal relationship with God that's not all about religion but focuses on relationship. When Samantha set out to seek a relationship with God, little did she know she was introducing others into relationship with Him as well.

Doing this interview, I recognized the truth that was my life:

"When you walk the tightrope without a net, you have no choice but to get to the other side, and there in that space is God waiting for you with open arms."

Have you ever had a point in time where you took a leap of faith, an action step that you just knew was not from you? It's called a leap of faith for a reason.

When you live your life with God at the helm, everything will flow and you're not striving; all the pieces just come together.

Life should not be about striving and surviving but about thriving and that's the difference when He is in it. My experience is, I think it, I say it, I declare it and He puts it inside me and I say, okay, God I guess this is where we are going.

When it flows like a gentle stream graciously moving around everything in its path – even the boulders – you can assume it's from God. Those areas of resistance, may not be where He will have you go. Something to think about.

Samantha wanted a spiritual experience and not a religious one and she got more than she could have ever dreamed of. People who have the heart of heaven can see the heart of "Li'l Bit of Heaven too;" people who have the heart of heaven see it as a spiritual hospital, an incubator, and the ministry that it is.

Hundreds of thousands of people came through these doors from all over the globe: Scotland, Australia, Africa, Israel, Afghanistan, Estonia, India, England just to name a few. They just came from all over; guest speakers, musicians, authors, and even though "A Lil bit of Heaven" is not funded for hotels and travel, these people feel called to come.

One of Samantha's favorite guests was from Alaska. He was an Eskimo and he got up to sing an Eskimo worship song. Samantha jested with him that he walked in looking like someone right out of the pages of *National Geographic* with big bone structure and leathery skin. The essence of "Samantha's Li'l bit of Heaven" became that very thing – an opening and an understanding of each person's uniqueness unto themselves while yet all of us being the same.

The transformation that is Samantha's reward is someone who did not know Jesus became a woman who not only walks with God, but actually fulfilling their life's purpose and their life's calling through Him! Samantha has seen people go from suicidal to saved; from so very lost to gracefully found.

She gets to see people get that they are not only saved from their trials on earth, but also for all eternity. What a joy and what a blessing. At "Samantha's Li'l bit of Heaven," people are friends outside of there, doing business together, and fellowship together, as well.

There's a freedom here – a freedom to be who you are and to come as you are; there's no, "You have to do this or you have to do that;" it's like a representation of Jesus; come one and come all.

It's a trickle-down effect that has, and still does, after 20 years have an impact on hundreds of thousands; all because a woman named Samantha decided to ask the tough questions and she not only got the answers she was seeking for herself, but she graciously shared them with the world. Now that deserves an Amen!

Samantha's Lesson:

Things you don't understand and don't want to happen, happen sometime anyway. When you seek God and turn to him, He can use it for your highest good.

Samantha's Blessing:

Sometimes those very things you deem as "bad" are the very thing God is preparing to bless you with. It might be an unfortunate and painful experience, but in seeking God out, sometimes He will use it for your good. Samantha's painful experience along with her relentless inquiry of seeking God led her to be one of the biggest contributions in ministry ever to exist on Long Island, New York; all on the favor and promise of God.

So Be It: Amen!

www.samanthaslilbitofheaven.org

CHAPTER FOURTEEN
ARE YOU TALKING TO ME?
THERE ARE NO COINCIDENCES

The first time I walked into Samantha's Li'l bit of Heaven I met Samantha. She was warm and welcoming and enveloped me from the moment I walked in the door. I chatted with her briefly about my coming to know the Lord and she and I connected immediately. I told her I felt called into writing in ministry, but there was no way I would honor that; I wasn't good enough.

She jokingly said to me I was pulling the Moses card – where God calls him to do something and he says no, not me, I'm not equipped. Samantha went on to say, those who were not equipped were the exact people He was seeking. I shared with Samantha immediately after hearing this voice about being called to ministry in writing, I said no I'm not good enough; I don't have a degree.

Additionally, I had made an inquiry to Liberty University a while before this and during the week I had received a postcard saying, "God does not call the equipped, He equips the obedient." God was nodding.

It was time for Samantha's speaker to come onto the stage so she and I sat adjacent to each other. I was there with my mom who was in her late eighties back then. The speaker got up to the small wooden stage and began his presentation. The first thing out of his mouth was something similar to "Have you ever thought you heard the voice of the Holy Spirit call you into ministry and you thought to yourself, "I'm not good enough.'" Samantha looked at me and I looked at her and we both just had our mouths open. Samantha will attest this truly did happen. She wrote me a note on a sticky pad, which I still have to this day. The note said, "Ann, this is one of those, Dear Ann from God, I love you moments."

The Lesson:

God loves me so much even though I'm having a hard time being obedient to Him. He continues to bless me unconditionally because He truly believes in the power He has created in me. He knows what I'm capable of and He knows where I'm weak; He continues to do the work in me. I look into the poison of procrastination even with writing this book because procrastination allows me to avoid perfectionism. If I don't do it, I can't fail. If I don't do it, no one can blame me for how good or not so good it is; if I can't face that it is imperfect, I don't have to fear its imperfection either. I don't have to worry and there's no space for, "I'm not good enough."

If you're like most people, then you'll be comforted to know that there are many of us that suffer from "I'm not good enough syndrome." Think about this deep limiting subconscious belief. God created you.

When we stand in our own power, knowing full well that our inherent gifts and talents are His gifts to us, we can then open those gifts and use them.

The Blessing:

The Blessing is within the Gifts: When I say "gifts," I'm not speaking of gifts that come out of a school book or that are attached to a title, degree, or any number of letters after your name. I'm talking about spiritual gifts.

Some of us have the gift of leadership and others have the gift of assisting brilliantly. Some of us were born with creative and artistic talents while others can stand in integrity in everything they do.

When you go into the thought process of not being good enough or being fearful, this is something from the enemy known as the mind. Your mind wants you to play it safe; playing it safe means no humiliation; no fear of failure, no fear of leaving the comfort zone, no danger.

It's our mind's business to keep us safe, but it's our higher self's business to thank that part of ourselves and let them know that you appreciate the thought (and thought is exactly what it is), but it's not always so necessary. We can do this, and we can survive on our own accord - mistakes and all - and we don't always have to live in fear of making a mistake or getting it wrong. That's called life.

When you live life mistakes and all, you live life full out.

You're human; humans make mistakes. I like to call it "silly human stuff." Let yourself off the hook. Guilt and shame are only good for in-the-moment experiences to let you know something doesn't feel right. Those emotions have no value for past mistakes; there's no going back and no room for regrets so why bother with them? Look at your present moment. Are you feeling guilty because of a current issue or is it old stuff coming back up to bite you? Is there something in your life right now that you need to take another look at and recreate because of guilt and shame or is there something past-based from your childhood there?

If you feel that feeling of not being good enough, just remember one thing and one thing only. God creates us in His likeness and image and He is perfect; so give glory to God.

You can Honor God by Honoring Your Gifts.

Trust in Him; don't trust in the voice of negativity that keeps you safe and keeps you playing small. Trust in God's great plan for you; move forward each and every day and move forward towards God's will for you and your life. If God didn't think you were good enough, He would've passed you by Himself.

We all Have Different Gifts we Bring to the Table; His Table.

CHAPTER FIFTEEN
A CHRISTMAS MIRACLE; YOU CAN'T MAKE THIS STUFF UP

It was Christmas, 2015. A Long Island family was on their way to New Hampshire for a family holiday road trip. They were busy prepping for the trip, checking out the car: tire pressure, oil change, windshield fluid, lights, etc. Suddenly, the husband noticed something odd on his block.

Two oil repair trucks were down at the home of their 95-year-old neighbor's house. Being a good neighbor and a good person, he went on down to check out the scene and ask what was up.

The repair man told him the elder's hot water pipe under the sink was broken for about two weeks. There was steam and mold on the walls and they were going to shut off the water and call Social Services, and have him taken away to be put in a home.

The neighbor asked if there was any way to stop the leak since it wasn't spurting hot water anywhere, just the steam. The repairmen were concerned about the mold. Taking it one more inquiry further, the neighbor questioned why they just couldn't use masks and stop the steam and get a cleanup crew in there for the mold. The response was pretty cut and dry, with a no as the final answer. They were just going to shut the water off for the time being and have the elder moved to a nursing home.

He contacted another neighbor; both of them had experience with shutting off leaks, as they fixed this kind of stuff all the time.

There was something heart-wrenching about a 95-year-old man going into a home on Christmas Eve. It was Friday and the neighbor and his family wouldn't be returning from holiday travel until Monday. He decided his next plan of action would be to, at the very least, return home early on Sunday, clean up the elder's home as best he could and help the elder get back home that much sooner.

It was like a sauna in the house on that Christmas Eve, the doors wouldn't close, and the carpet was saturated with footsteps full of water. There was steam coming out from under the sink, and the older gentleman's white tee shirt was discolored to brown from the steam.

They offered him to stay at their place with food, television, and heat with a sense of normalcy. The older man wanted to stay in his house and fight for his right to be there. What a situation.

He didn't know what else to do. It was time for mass so this neighbor went over to church and put a special intention on the prayer card. He put the address of the elder's home on the prayer card and asked for prayers for a Christmas miracle.

He signed his name and said as he handed it in to the usher, "This will never ever happen; it's just impossible."

Well, with God nothing is impossible. This neighbor had to prepare for his family trip and, with no other solution in sight, was truly upset about his friend and neighbor having to be sent to a home; he didn't want to leave his home.

What happens next is truly a Christmas miracle. The other neighbor, in the true spirit of Christianity, instead of spending time with his wife and children for Christmas, went over to the elder's home, took a snow shovel and shoveled nine large construction bags full of debris out of the hallways and put them to the curb. He had a friend who just happened to be a mold remediator; got his friend to come over and the remediator offered all the equipment for free. The only out-of-pocket expense was to pay the workers coming in on Christmas Day.

Not only that, he wouldn't take money from anyone else, not even his own church to help pay the elder's bill for the cleanup, the clothes or the rest of the supplies.

The neighbor went on to put a new faucet in the sink and in the bathroom, turned the water back on, got industrial machinery to remove the moisture from the house. The workers micro-scrubbed the house and walls to get the mold off.

That brown tee shirt which was supposed to be white – the neighbor went to Burlington Coat Factory and bought new clothes for the elder. Even the elder's shoes were green from mold.

As the original neighbor heard about the story, he broke down in tears because he thought it was something that could never happen on such a busy holiday like Christmas. But what better holiday above and beyond all others would a miracle occur?

He asked his neighbor how much he spent, but he was so humble; not accepting any money from anyone. All he said was that it didn't matter.

The only thing is, though, it did matter – it mattered to the 95-year-old elder. These neighbors and this elder, himself, are the true meaning of what a Christmas miracle is really all about; not from any movie or script, but in real life on a real day of glory, giving, and Godliness.

The Lesson:

Never say never when it comes to what God is capable of, especially on the day of all days, Christmas Day. Never underestimate the kindness, compassion or depth of human nature – especially in the worst of times.

The Blessing:

One man's ability to go above, beyond, and through a tragedy, as he quietly and humbly did God's work. He represented not only the true meaning of Christmas that Christmas Day, but he represented Christ himself.

CHAPTER SIXTEEN
OH DEER! I CAN FINALLY GRIEVE

During the battle of my spiritual journey (was I spiritual or was I religious?), there came a time where I couldn't think anymore. I couldn't choose and I couldn't decide. What was right, what was wrong, which way was up? So I chose not to decide. I chose to feel my way through what was right – for me.

After my Dad passed away, it took me some time to grieve, but when it happened, the flood gates of pain and sorrow opened up.

When my dad passed, my brother and my son went to the funeral parlor to make sure everything was in order. My brother was exploring the inquiry of whether or not to put pics up on my dad's photo board of his deer hunting days in order not to offend anyone. On the way to the funeral parlor, my son and my brother saw a buck run across the highway. It was the middle of the day. I can't say either one of them are really all that spiritual or not, but this did have an impact on both of them.

One night, I went to a service (sermon was about how the spirit joyfully leaves the body through death to join God) and I saw my friend Kathy. I met Kathy last year at a seminar teaching about Christ.

I still had questions. Was this a religious teaching, was it the truth, how strong was my faith. When I left the lady's house where the seminar was being held, there were two deer running wild in front of my car (in St. James, Long Island). First the buck and then the doe.

On the night of the service, I asked Kathy about the notice in the bulletin about needing assistance for worship service in nursing homes. She asked me if I would ever consider taking it over...WHAT? who me???

Anyhow, I asked her where it was - it was in the same nursing home where my dad was last.

(P.S. I had taken a seminar on commitment the year before, and I taped the homework assignment to my bedroom wall. One of the categories was volunteering and it says "to JOYFULLY volunteer with the elderly.").

So, I had dad on my mind that night...and I spoke to him out loud while driving home on the dark, twisting road that connected the back ends of both neighborhoods between the church and my home, "Dad, I miss you. I can FINALLY say that I miss you." I began to sob and I asked him what to do about my spirit mate. Was this right, was it wrong, what does God want me to do, what about our strange connections? No sooner than I made these inquiries, two deer ran in front of my car on that winding, heavily wooded road.

Am I making meaning out of all this? Yes! you bet I am. My dad was sending me a message...many messages.

And, that night...just for a little while...I got to be a little girl hugging her pillow who misses her dad. I got to cry my heart out then because I really did miss him. I could finally let go and grieve, and it's all good.

The Lesson:

It is neither right nor wrong to listen, look for, and be open to the signs. The signs are there to soothe you, to guide you, and simply to let you know, you are supported and loved. There's nothing much wrong with this.

The Blessing:

The blessing came when I stopped denying grief and I just allowed it. Allowing grief was healing. It was like breathing in ocean air. Grief had to work its way through me so it could make its way out of me to the other side.

What is on the other side of grief? Joy, lessons, memories and love.

CHAPTER SEVENTEEN
THE ANGEL GABRIEL

As my father drew closer and closer to his heavenly respite, one aide after another came to our home. One quit, the other fired, and so it went. We finally received an aide that was an absolute angel. I never got his name though. I asked my mom and she laughed and confessed she did not know his name either.

Every day, he tried to grab a hold of me and ask to talk with me. I was either running in or running out to work, with the kids, to a social services meeting for my dad or to school.

Finally, he persisted and had his way. I agreed to speak with him. I had to confess to him though, that I did not know his name, but thought so highly of him that my mother and I thought he was an angel – he finally told me his name and, yes, it was Gabriel.

His message for me was that he was not here for my father, but he was here for me. He and I had something to accomplish together. I told him my newfound interest in the Bible and he just so happened to be a minister from Nigeria, as well.

As of this writing, I can say there is room for improvement in my Bible reading endeavors. I google search, I read the Bible, when my mom was alive and still with me this year, we would start many of our mornings off by reading the Book of Psalms. I grieve for that now. She only passed two weeks ago. I'm not ready to grieve her fully, but, like with my dad, when it comes it will come like a tidal wave knocking me to the ground and spinning my world upside down.

I grieved so much as I prepared, but am staying in denial in this moment. I was her caregiver; she was my mommy.

Although her passing is horrible for me, I know she gave me the gift of life – not once, but twice. She is giving new life to me and allowing me to recreate myself once again.

In death, there is new life. I'm stepping out of the role of caregiver for the last 24 years and stepping into the role of empowered, talented, successful and creative woman. Who am I? No longer the mom I used to be as I pack up my youngest birdie and help prepare her to leave the nest and no longer have earthly parents, the more important questions is – who will I become?

A new adventure awaits. I kick and scream and dive into the icy waters of the unknown, learn how to keep my body temperature up and keep swimming. Learn how to maneuver the waters, float for a while, then keep swimming forward, jumping on board a yacht to eat gourmet food, drink fine wine and meet new people – hey, if you're going to create stuff why not let it be good!

No matter what, though, it's important for me to give you this message; you're not alone – you're never alone. There are heavenly angels and then there are those earth angels that God, Himself, sends your way to help you out of this sometimes heart-wrenching thing called life.

The Lesson:

When you think you are all alone, know this for certain – God will never forsake and abandon you. It may seem like you are all alone, but believe me this is only your mind playing games with you. It is not the truth!

God will always provide the right person, place and time for everything and if He doesn't, He will provide a way out. Pay attention to the signs and you will be guided and directed accordingly.

The Blessing:

When you choose faith, you choose it all – the blessings, the way out and the way up. When you walk around truly believing God will provide an answer, a way or a means, it will always be there waiting for you – one step ahead. All you have to do is catch up to it, that's all.

CHAPTER EIGHTEEN
AN ORDINARY TRIP TO THE CLINIC; OR IS IT?

When you wake up every day, it seems like just another ordinary day, doesn't it? Sometimes those ordinary days throw us a curve. Shocking events occur sometimes on days when we think all is calm and well. When there's no place left to go, and you have nothing left to give, sometimes you have to give it up – to God.

Here's a story of an extraordinary woman who had an extraordinary chain of events.

It was Labor Day 2014 and she was heading to a friend's house for a barbeque. It was also the day of the 2nd anniversary of her mom's passing so she headed out to the cemetery too.

Not feeling well, she made her way back and stopped in at a walk-in clinic. Her assumption was to run in really quickly and run out just as quickly to check on a possible urinary tract infection. Really simple stuff, right? Not so fast.

The doctor saw something more than just a traditional urinary tract infection (uti); she noticed there was pain on the right side and had a concern for potential appendicitis.

"I'm sending you for a CT scan right now," weren't the words this woman wanted to hear at the moment. All she wanted to hear was she was going to get a quick-fix antibiotic and go on her merry way to her barbeque. With instructions to drink the necessary liquid before the CT scan, she was on her way for an emergency CT scan; and it was Labor Day weekend. This now became a game of good news/bad news and, unfortunately, the bad news was awful.

When the technician bid her farewell and told her to enjoy the weather, she immediately sensed a tone in the technician's voice; it wasn't just a pleasant, "Have a nice day." There was more to it, she could feel it in her gut.

The CT scan showed something on her uterus and she was told to address it immediately. She was told to call her ob/gyn to address the results in person. With her mind racing, she called the ob/gyn and they took her in immediately. This was spiraling from bad to worse.

When she got to the doctor's office, there was a recommendation for a biopsy. Of course, her first question was to ask the doctor if she thought it was cancer. The doctor didn't know at this point, but wanted to make sure, just in case.

The waiting felt endless as she tried to keep her mind occupied. Sometimes, the waiting is the worst part; the not knowing is sometimes more frightening than having the disease itself. Not knowing if you have cancer, not knowing if you will recover from cancer, not knowing what your future looks like.

As she waited and time went by, she thought maybe no news was good news. Unfortunately for her, this was not the case. She was told she had grade 1 cancer; the results say slow-growing and non-aggressive.

For her, the first coincidence was thinking she had an ordinary urinary tract infection and going to the clinic on the same date of the two-year anniversary of her mom's death.

The second coincidence came from the doctor herself.

By October, she had a radical hysterectomy, six rounds of chemo and 25 radiation treatments. She followed up with oncology every three months. Shortly after, she thought she might have another urinary tract infection and back to the clinic again she went and lo and behold.

The original clinic doctor who sent her for an emergency CT scan saw her. She asked the doctor if she remembered her, and she told the doctor she had probably saved her life with the extra step CT scan. All she wanted was a "hit-and-run" antibiotic and to go to a barbeque. They hugged and hugged. Of course, the doctor remembered her.

The doctor commented she didn't know what it was that made her think something else was wrong, but something else told her to send her patient off for the further testing. Typically, in a clinic setting, the business is to get people in and out, but this day would change two lives.

The doctor prayed to God to allow her to listen to someone that day, to truly hear someone and listen to them and help heal them.

Because of her, this doctor comes to work every day and says a prayer to God. She prays to God to please help her to listen – truly listen – to every single patient; let her listen to them and what their needs are.

The doctor kneels in prayer every night; God, I hope by listening I save a life or helped someone today. She attributes this second coincidence as God having done the work and answering her prayer.

Throughout her surgery and her treatments, this wonderful and faithful woman of God would ask those treating her if they believed in the power of prayer and each time, the answer was always a resounding yes with no hesitation.

During her surgery, there was a discovery of a poppy-sized piece of cancer. Her husband says if the doctor would've sneezed, he would've missed it and attributes the grace of God for allowing the doctor to discover it.

During treatment, there was no nausea, fatigue and no burning sensation as she was afraid of, only healing under way. She truly believes God was nodding at her because it serves as a message to other women.

The Lesson:

To pay attention to those signs and symptoms when you don't feel well and don't try to squeeze appropriate health care into a busy schedule. Take time to listen to your body.

The Blessing:

Being a woman of faith, God had matched her up with the right person at the right time; another woman of faith who had prayed that very same day for God to help her save someone. God answered with a powerful, graceful, and mighty yes! Where regular protocol medicine in the form of pap smears, and internal exams did not show anything wrong previously, this miracle occurred because two women of faith came together at the right place and in the right time.

CHAPTER NINETEEN
DRAGONFLIES, LADY BUGS, AND PENNIES; OH MY!

During my interviews with people and along the journey, I cannot tell you how many times people have told me stories of receiving signs. Some see lady bugs while, for others, it's dragonflies.

One young girl would see a dragonfly whenever her grandfather came to conversation and another woman saw lady bugs when she felt deeply connected to her twin flame.

And yet for others still, it's pennies – pennies from heaven. I had asked God to allow me to close out 2015 with healing. Be careful what you ask for, because without pain you can't have healing.

I had come full circle with my spirit mate; I felt peaceful and grateful for the lessons I learned and ready to move on like a rocket ship recently fueled up. What happened next was unfortunate, like something out of a bad drama movie.

I had become friends with one of his exes – only thing is, I didn't know she was one of his exes, but found out the hard way. She was so much like me in many ways. I considered her and even called her my soul sister. The coincidences and serendipities were uncanny. If I didn't know any better, I'd swear I knew her from a past life, had I even believed in such a notion.

When I discovered the truth, I began to coach her from all I had learned from my journey. No one would argue with me, not my friends or family who knew me and most certainly not my spirit mate – I did the work. Not only did I do the work of transformation, I did the hard work where I put all my blood, sweat and tears into every painful footstep until I arrived at the destination. That destination was me. I took responsibility for my life. I learned I could create it however I wanted it to show up. Now that's empowering.

What I came to discover just before the New Year was that this friendship wasn't a healthy relationship any longer. I no longer needed to get caught up in drama, untruths, and withholding of information. I didn't want to be that kind of woman or be with that kind of woman. The friendship had run its course and the relationship had to end.

Want to know something though? God loves me so much he sent me a wondrous and delightfully delicious sign not even 10 minutes after the New Year. I was out with my cousin and her best friend. Her best friend spent quite some time telling me stories of how she finds pennies when she thinks of her dad.

It was 12:10, I took off my shoes and decided to dance into the New Year gleefully and joyfully and most especially in spite of what had occurred. As I looked down, there on the floor was a shiny brand new penny! It was so significant because it was symbolic for me. Not only would this all be behind me soon enough, I would come out polished and new just as God intended! God sometimes puts us through the furnace to polish us like fine gold. Know what? This was one of the biggest lessons and best blessings in my life.

The Lesson:

The lesson came in the form of learning how to use my head and my heart. You know how they say to follow your heart? Well, all my life I did that and it got me nothing but trouble.

Then, I tried using my head to analyze and think and make logic out of things but analysis/paralysis didn't work either. You know what's even better?

The Blessing:

At 53 years of age, I've learned to use both my head and my heart and, for me, that's divinity. Incorporating both my logical mind and my heartfelt intuition from my heart are leading my ship and guiding my missile. I'm connected to source through both. I feel divine.

When I ask myself a question and can't find the answer, somehow it usually turns out that the answer is "both." I can be spiritual and religious. I can be logical and intuitive. I can be intelligent and creative. I can give myself attention and I can receive the warm fuzzies from others too for good reasons.

It doesn't have to be one or the other; it can be both. So stop beating yourself up and allow yourself to be a complex, complicated, delicious and delightful human being. The answer isn't always one or the other. See where you can find an area of your life where you can be "both."

The blessing was the biggest blessing yet. I had opportunity to take action; I didn't. I got to stand in my integrity to who I am in this world. I got to keep my sense of self. I got to raise my bar and not lower myself. I got to walk away with my head held proud.

While endings are never sought after, sometimes they are necessary. Sometimes God will remove a relationship from you that is not for your highest good and you must allow Him to do this work in your life. As women, we must learn we are responsible for our choices as adults. It's no longer our parents fault, our childhood, or the men in our lives either. It is sometimes just the stories inside our heads we tell ourselves – that somehow we are not good enough. We all, fellow sisters, are good enough – as is – just the way we are. We all bring something different to the table – His table.

CHAPTER TWENTY
GOD DELIVERS

A Note Inside a Library Book

All along my journey, I kept playing ping pong with my emotions. One minute I was empowered and the next minute I was feeling the "I'm not good enough" story.

Who else but the divine could orchestrate what happens next? I take a book out of the library; I'm feeling lower than low. I don't have a fully completed degree, I'm a single mom, I'm a caregiver. All I have is this raw talent and passion for writing and helping others; where am I going to go and what am I going to do with that?

At the library, I take out a book – I'd be lying if I said I could remember the name right now, but it could have possibly been one about the different love languages. In any event, in the middle of reading this book, no joke, there was a note inside.

It was a handwritten note reading, "Success is making the most of who you are with what you already have." What??? I looked around and over my shoulder. It wasn't until I looked up, however, that I realized it was a divine message. What are the odds of receiving a note on a sore subject where you need some beautiful healing? When God Nods, the odds are always in your favor.

A Postcard

During one of my many moments of, "I'm not good enough" (sounds like a broken record at this point), I kept telling myself I am not equipped educationally to write in ministry – even though I felt strongly called to do so. My writing wouldn't allow me to not pursue this path and my soul knew it was going to come to fruition. My head, however, was on an ego trip of trying to protect me, it, and my "self" from leaving the comfort and safety of "the comfort zone."

By the way, the comfort zone – it's overrated anyway. Trying to decode my next strategic move, I received a postcard from Liberty University saying something to the effect, "God does not call the equipped, He calls the obedient." Well, I got told – there it was in black in white, a message from God to believe in myself and believe in Him more importantly. His will for my life was about to unfold. Is anything too difficult for the almighty? No, I sheepishly admit.

Here I am today, published three books and poetry, went back to school, started my own business, created an inspiring business for caregivers, and there's more. There's the newspaper article, the online television show, the offers to do marketing events and book signings along with teaching journaling at support groups. A caregiver's support group and hosting events for caregivers sound like lovely creations, as well. All this because of something more important than I'd ever realized – no degree or title in the world can equate to having a heart full of compassion and a heart after God along with the embracing of your true spiritual gifts without all the noise of looking good and fear of being seen.

Even on Social Media?

On more than one occasion and in the deepest and darkest moments of my life, I've plugged into social media and seen the perfect meme, read the right story or found an answer I didn't even know I was searching for just yet.

God knows when to direct and where to direct you. As long as you continue to seek him and search, the answers will appear. Yes, there are times when God says no. There are also times when you feel God is nowhere in the mix. If you've ever felt this way, I can assure you, it's just a matter of learning how to depend on yourself for a little while, make your own choices and reap the rewards or suffer the repercussions of those choices.

Sometimes God will send you the signs, but it's up to you to follow along on the journey or fall off the beaten path for a little while. It's called being human. Sometimes we are tested to see if we are ripe for the next event and it's okay if we are not; it just means until next time. God is busy and has many jobs for just as many people. If you're not the right man for the job, it's okay. Everybody has their spiritual weaknesses and strengths and God knows exactly how to use them all.

God is not waving a magic wand and orchestrating your life all by himself; however, He is ready and available to come home to when you don't exactly get it perfect. It's in those moments of fear, failure, and fright when God will step in and offer His most perfect gift – the gift of forgiveness.

There are articles I've been lead to read, quotes I needed to see and books I needed to buy as long as I stayed in the place and space of seeking, the answers were there waiting for me to arrive all the while.

Whatever man may make, God can and will use it for your highest good. If you're open to receive, He is more than happy to deliver – even if it's in the form of a tweet or a post.

The Lesson:

You never know when God is going to nod at you, but always be open and expect it. God will use any means and way to send you some love.

The Blessing:

Share your testimony, share your story and smile with someone else when these things happen; you never know, they might say, "Oh, you too?"

CHAPTER TWENTY-ONE
A "DEFINING" MOMENT

If we are lucky, we all have a moment where life leaves us with our mouths wide open – in a good way, that is. I'm happy to say I had one of those moments. My highest and most spiritual friends disappointed me at the same time not keeping their word to me and I could not understand why I was still single; so I had a conversation out loud and personal with God.

God, do I not have any value or worth with my spiritual friends? Deciding not to go down a deep and dark path, I opened up one of my books from a class I was taking. The instructor recommended Merriam Webster Dictionary. That day, I had told my spiritual friends I was considering writing a blog called, "Divine Serendipity."

Upon typing in the web address for the dictionary, the site came up with the photo contest of the week with instructions to match any photo to the word of the week. The word was Serendipity! The photo was a picture of two jets crossing over the other leaving a streak in the sky making the sign of the cross.

There it was! Divine Serendipity at its finest. Knowing God was speaking, I continued. Embarrassed as I am to admit it, I "Googled" women of value and worth because this was the original conversation I just had with God.

A link came up with an article written by men on their interpretation of a woman's value and worth. Oh, this I had to read! The website showed no indication of being spiritual or even Christian. The first sentence read something like, "Hey, you, yes you the one reading this. Do not think for a minute you are here by mistake. You are here for a reason."

"The only dictionary you need to define value and worth is the dictionary Christ left behind. Do not define your value and worth on whether or not a man is pursuing you. You are the daughter of a King and therefore you are a princess." God could not have spoken to me any clearer or made me feel his tight hugs of comfort and reassurance any better or stronger.

HE loves me. God loves me for He created me and He did not make any mistakes. I truly feel and believe in my own value and worth, mistakes, sins and all, since that divine moment. Don't get me wrong, I falter and I fall hard in this department, but I eventually return to a steadfast belief of value and worth.

Now I go around saying out loud, "I am always in the right place at the right time!"

The Lesson:

Short and sweet: Be curious; be open to seeking answers and somewhere in the mix, you will find the truth.

The Blessing:

When you are resourceful, you seek out the questions; when you seek out the questions, the answers eventually come. So be it!

CHAPTER TWENTY-TWO
ABUNDANCE – EVEN IN THE BATHROOM THERE'S SIGNS?

Sometimes I think God has a sense of humor. He knows how, when and where to get our attention some time. But, in the bathroom? I had started seeing a counselor to help me navigate my way through single life and the repetitive patterns I had with the not-exactly-right kinds of men I was attracting in my life.

On one particular visit, my counselor could not understand why her abundance bead bracelet had just exploded on her wrist this day. It seemed as though it just jumped off her wrist. That is, until I came in and told her I was about to take a new journey in my writing career and it was a big day for me. She told me she understood now what she was supposed to do. She had collected all the beads up from the bathroom floor earlier in the day and put them in a tea cup. She handed me two. She asked me to wash her "self" off the beads and to keep them in a special place on my person. She said there were no more beads, she collected them all.

I went into the bathroom to wash them off and there on the sink was another bead waiting for me. Two weeks later, on my follow up visit, I found two more beads on the bathroom floor. The janitor of the building had been in several times to clean, yet two more abundance beads were waiting for me. They all sit in a velvet box on my desk.

The Lesson:

I'm the only one in the way of creating my own abundance. Abundance is mine if I am open to find it. Don't forget to look in unexpected places!

The Blessing:

When you are excited and exhilarated about a new opportunity and you share it with others, your enthusiasm is contagious. The right people, your tribe, will be more than happy not only to share your joy but to bless you with beads of abundance along the way.

CHAPTER TWENTY-THREE
A STROKE OF LUCK

There's an old saying about making lemonade when life throws you lemons. Well, for ReneMarie, she did more than make lemonade. She turned her bowl of lemons into many different juicy and delectable recipes, from lemon zest tea to lemon meringue pie. Anyone else in her shoes may have given up, but instead, ReneMarie showed up and stepped up. Her story is nothing short of amazing.

ReneMarie knows the truth of who she is and wishes to share her testimony here in this space. She wants everyone to know this is available to them, as well. She says we all know the truth of who we are supposed to be. When you are open to receive, you see the many signs of that experience. You get to live your dream as long as you are willing to keep on going.

She is no stranger to struggle and strife and her story will amaze and inspire you. One such example is remembering the early phases of single parenthood. When she had to send her kids off with their father, she broke down in the shower just sitting on the floor. Her heart was breaking in the worst form; life had changed with her children. She was crying and had to give it up to God, telling him she couldn't do this anymore. That was one of many darker moments she considered unbearable.

When she thinks back and wonders, how did she get through it, her answer is through the grace of God. The big moment, however, in ReneMarie's life came from a devastating illness.

She turned that illness into a ministry. Here's her astonishing yet inspiring story.

With a background as a softball coach and player, ReneMarie is aware of how those first seven innings of the game of life prepare you for what's to come next. One of her many intentions going forward is to coach and speak to young children and athletes on how the principle of softball helps in the game of real life.

Back in 1976, she was in the game and on the field. Her softball coach at the time put her in the suicide squeeze in order to bring home a win for the team. Now, you must understand something about ReneMarie; when she does something – she's all in. There's nothing halfway about her. During the game, she was dashing home from third plate. Unfortunately, her helmet flew off and, as the batter dropped the bat, her foot hit the end of the bat and it hit her in the back of the head.

She began going into convulsions. At this point in time, she didn't hear the voice of God yet, but she does say she always had something different about her. She floated through life with a vibrant love for people. There was always a desire to make people happy and a strong belief in God.

Although she had suffered a concussion, she was allowed to go home and, true to form, wanted to play in the next game. Of course, her coach couldn't allow her. She had to sit out for three games. She couldn't stay still and was determined to be a part of the game, so her coach had her coach first base.

What happens next is amazing. 13 years to the day – to the exact day - on the same field and with the same people surrounding her, the unthinkable happened. She was heading back to the dugout and she heard God speak to her saying, "I'm going to try this again." She took a few steps, walking across the field and onto the dugout, when she suddenly collapsed. Her baby was only six months old at the time; ReneMarie had suffered a stroke.

In retrospect, she believes with all her heart God was trying to get her attention back then in 1976 and she wasn't listening. She felt she was too determined, too focused about life. If you gave her something to accomplish, she went for it straight on, which is why God chose her – to give her a purpose and something to work on. One thing about ReneMarie, if you gave her a purpose, you know undoubtedly it will be accomplished.

She felt lifted out of her body and watched everything happen below; she was viewing her experience from a third person point of view, from the ride in the ambulance on the way to the hospital to seeing her father at the foot of the bed watching her.

She had a knowing, she heard a voice and she took a journey toward heaven. She says of her experience that you just know it's heaven. It's so surreal and loving and heaven is just this place - an aura of love; there is nothing wrong in heaven. The love is so powerful; she was taken to heaven and she looked up and saw the light and heard a voice, call her name, "Rene."

She responded, "What do you want?" and she just knew it was God.

It wasn't as much a place as it was a knowing for her in her experience. She begged God, "I'm not done; please God, don't take me." The reply astonished her, "I don't want to take you; I just wanted to get your attention." ReneMarie always knew God was with her, in her, and around her, but she didn't converse with Him. She just knew God was with her always, and that was pretty much it for her, until this happened.

She remembers begging God to put her back into her body and promising to do whatever it was He wanted her to do. He honored her request because He had plans and a purpose for her and for her life. When people hear her story, they tend to think her life would be rosy after this happening; however, this was not the case. Her life was full of struggle, but that, she came to later realize was exactly how God intended to bless her. Her trial became her testimony.

She had work to do physically and mentally, as well as recover from aphasia. While other people may have become angered with God, not ReneMarie. She says to this day, she trusts Him. To the contrary, there was an inner voice that told her she needed to be doing something. That something was to become an advocate for others suffering from strokes and aphasia. And what an advocate she has become indeed!

After only a short while, she began to really understand what her purpose was; she didn't doubt God or question him. For her, there's an inner voice. It tells her whether or not she should be doing something. She knew this is what she needed to do.

Right from the start, she was all in for her recovery. She would ask her physical therapist, "Okay, what do I need to do to recover; I'm here."

She was shocked and surprised that she had a stroke – initially she didn't even comprehend it, I had a stroke – what is a stroke – it was a third leading cause of death. There's not too much knowledge about strokes and not a lot of noise about it either. It's often associated with older people.

Since she been in this world of stroke and aphasia, she met a little girl who suffered a stroke and a woman whose child had a stroke in uterus; strokes can happen to anybody at any time no matter what and it changes your life in one split second.

She goes on to point out if you know the signs, you can save a life. ReneMarie walks with her leg dragging a bit behind her, her right arm bent and her smile has changed as well. However, what's so inspiring about her is when she goes for a job interview or fills out an application and asked if disabled, without thinking or blinking she says, no, she is not disabled.

From the time after the stroke, her life evolved where she went on to create new things. She planted it in her brain, she had to do her own personal work and she had to peel away all layers of her personal issues existing in her life to get to the point to be free and clear and with no layers around her so she could go on to help others.

Her advice to anyone else – first and foremost is to listen. You have to go into silence every day, and that could be in the form of meditation or prayer. You have to find the silence. Most of us keep busy with noise in the real world all the time; we look at the television, we look at our phones and even when we are talking with someone, we are not quiet. We don't take a moment to listen, really listen.

When you have a conversation with God, you must be quiet and you cannot be in tune when you are noisy-minded. ReneMarie truly believes you have to believe in all the good and abundance God has for you, even if it shows up in a way you'd rather not have experienced.

I've learned the hard way, we don't understand the why of how God works, but in retrospect (what an amazing tool), we do get the privilege and the joy of seeing and saying, "Oh, that's why!" We may not like it at the time, but it is always for our highest good. All we have to do is believe.

ReneMarie agrees with me on this. She feels it's necessary to believe first and then call on God. She says trusting that God will slowly work with you is key. It's not like you suddenly have the ability to trust. She believes trust is earned; we have a relationship with God and when we are open to that relationship, we need to maintain it at all times.

Just like you have respect for your marriage and in friendship, bad things happen the way life is and the way the earth is. God will definitely help us through it and help us get to the other side.

She goes on to say we have to listen to the little tiny voice. She gives a perfect example in her next statement. Every person has the ability to tune in to His soft voice. If someone were yelling at you, would you listen? No, the person with the soft demeanor and gentle spirit is the one who gets your attention in a long-lasting way with positive effects. For her, when God speaks, He speaks in a quiet and gentle voice – the voice of unconditional love.

He talks gently and she quietly hears

When asked if she had any tips or techniques to hear God's calling upon our lives, she shares these tips:

- Be open and connected
- Do open meditation and carry that throughout your day
- Focus on that intention all through the day
- Don't always sit still when meditating (that's a new one!)
- Walk around the house, listen to music; you don't need to be quietly meditating
- She walks around visualizing, listening and asking God a question; asking her what to do next, where she should go; this helps her to continue her relationship with God

ReneMarie points out there are people who worship once per week and then the rest of the week aren't connected to God. Her belief is to pray, seek guidance, and to love God while reflecting on a way of life which continues throughout your day and your week.

Ask for forgiveness for things you've done wrong and you can practice what you are living into and what you believe. Live into who you want to be every single moment of your life and practice, practice, practice it daily.

ReneMarie practiced listening to God, and He knocked her into attention. On the subject of her long recovery from stroke, she points out she had angels in her life. She could see God in these earthbound angels because He was helping her to recover to learn lessons she had yet to learn and guiding her to this point in her life to become the amazing advocate for strokes and aphasia she is. She had become, through her trials, a stroke and aphasia advocate. She says, she works for God.

The Lesson:

Quiet and still your mind and believe first; everything will fall into alignment.

The Blessing:

ReneMarie created a foundation for stroke and aphasia awareness stemming from her own experience. She began doing telethons to raise money and awareness. She is a lover of purpose and helping others and music, as well. From as long as she could remember, she was fascinated and enthralled by the Jerry Lewis telethons from her childhood years.

She says of her telethon and charitable organization, one thing led to another and then to another. She listened to her angels and although it took a lot of work and determination, the vision came true. You must trust nothing happens without you pursuing it and you wanting to get it.

There are three purposes for her vision:

1. Stroke and aphasia awareness
2. Annual telethon

3. Help support those whose insurance runs out. She would love to see a future where there is a place to go – a center of sorts - when the insurance runs out and the families of strokes can come for help so they can get back to the business at hand – and that business is the business of loving their family members back to health and loving themselves as well.

Love is the answer to recovery she says with no doubt. When someone suffers you need to just love them through recovery – don't worry about anything else; they need the love.

She has questions though; how are the finances going to come to fruition to help bring awareness? God is already taking care of it all, she says confidently. It's so easy to get caught up in what doesn't work and focus on the wrong, but we can look for our own joys and focus on them instead; the rest will follow.

Life is not a bowl of cherries, but the small things are everything.

Because she's been in the place of darkness and not knowing what else to do, her testimony is beyond credible. She says, we are all here on earth trying to make it and trying to be kind, just trying to love one another. There's the joy. She says she's not ready to leave earth yet and wishes to get more done in a quiet, tranquil and calm manner. She feels it may be her next best approach rather than being busy, busy, busy all of the time.

For her, this is a principle to work on – juggle some things on the to-do list, get some accomplished and the rest, it's okay if they don't get done. She's learned the true art of letting go; she moves forward and what needs to get done, does, but in God's time – not hers.

God doesn't live by the clock. We are free to experience life and be in the moment, eager to see what happens next. Think about being a person who walks around wondering what next great thing will happen to move you along on the journey and you'll get some great insight to who ReneMarie truly is.

She says how you show up and who you want to be regardless of what you think or how you want to be perceived is how she really wants to live her life.

Here is a list of all of ReneMarie's achievements and what a list it is!

Rene Marie Testa Adams

Aphasia is a "silent" life changing effect of stroke or brain trauma

Did you know that nearly 80% of Strokes can be prevented?

Language of Love Telethon-April 9,2017

ReneMarie Language of Love Foundation INC

ReneMarie Stroke of Luck Internet TV Show

www.renemarielanguageoflove.org

www.languageoflovetelethon.org

www.renemariestrokeoflucktv.com

www.renemarieproductions2.com

renemarielanguageoflove@gmail.com

973-985-0420

CHAPTER TWENTY-FOUR
RIPPING OUT THE ROOTS, HANGING ON AND PULLING THE WEEDS

In the worst of times in my life where the change of life was upon me, (okay, a little personal but what the heck), I remember being fearful of the meds my doctor wanted to put me on. I didn't feel comfortable taking anything because there was no other "adult" to keep an eye out for me. I was anxious and distraught and feeling a little depressed, as well.

I clearly remember sitting there with my head in my hands and my heart in my mouth, "Dear God, where are you in all this? Why am I still single? Why am I alone and why am I going through these changes right now?" At that moment, I remember this feeling of darkness and dread come over me. I wondered if I was going to make it, who would save me from this time in my life. It wasn't passing soon enough and I'd already suffered for a few years.

Then all of a sudden I had a vision in my mind's eye. I saw the hand of God reach down into the pits of my gut and rip out an old limiting belief from my soul. It was my story of, "I'm not good enough." Just moments before I had decided in my mind the reason I was still single was because I was not good enough. I felt God rip that limiting belief right out of me. More significantly, I clearly remember a vision like it was just today, where I was hanging on to the end of that ugly, dark rooted weed and clinging to it for dear life.

"God, why are you taking my story away? I don't know anything else!" I saw God gently shake me off the end of those roots I so desperately wanted to hang on to and I landed on empty, barren land.

Breathlessly, I screamed at him, "Why are you leaving me here all alone without my story and my limiting belief. It's all I've ever known. You've left me here on barren ground."

To which He replied, "I've left you on fertile soil, a new clearing and a new place to sow."

The Lesson:

The longer you hold onto something God is trying to remove, the longer you and you alone delay the new crop God has in store for you.

> *You can view your situation as an ending*
> *or as a new place to plant on fertile soil.*
> *It's all a matter of perception.*

The Blessing:

I made it through the deepest, darkest and most difficult times of my life by keeping in relationship with God. I may not have loved what He was doing in the moment, but the new clearing was a place where I planted seeds of self-love, rows of value, and mounds of self-worth.

I came to realize that self-discipline, self-worth, self-esteem, self-confidence, and self-reliance all came from one source; and that source was me – my sense of self.

It was in the moment and time where I was at my lowest, needing to pull deeply into my faith when God decided it was the perfect time to remove the old and help me to create the new.

In my most vulnerable state was where I received the gift of surrender. I was willing to give it all up to God and let him take from me what would no longer serve me – or the people I came here to serve.

CHAPTER TWENTY-FIVE
ALWAYS IN THE RIGHT PLACE AT THE RIGHT TIME

I could write another 100 pages about coincidences and serendipities, but I won't do it here; however, I'd like to leave you with a few more of the most poignant and memorable coincidences I've experienced. I'll end this book with a few more stories which will surely entertain and enlighten you.

He Who is Last is First

It was 6:00 a.m.; I was having a panic attack. How was I going to take care of both my aging parents, be a single mom and help my daughter get into college, go to work, beside everything else in my life? I was living into the unwelcome spirit of overwhelm.

I picked up the Bible and opened it to Matthew 20:16, "So the last will be first and the first will be last." It was Sunday that day. I went to church and sure enough the pastor chose this Bible verse to speak about on this particular day. God was nodding.

On more than one occasion, I searched for answers and for truths and on opening the Bible randomly, there it was – the truth I was seeking. You can't make this up. On many occasions, it wasn't what I wanted to hear, but sometimes the truth never is.

God Taps Me on the Shoulder

When my roof was leaking, my pool broke down, the computer was not working, my car was going in for repairs and even my toilet (yes, my toilet) decided it was a good time to act up as well, I thought I would all but lose my mind when the television set chose to jump in on the party.

This happened all in the span of one day; it all fell apart and so did I. Sitting there on my steps sobbing, I chastised God – if you want me to write for you in ministry, then you need to meet me half way – give me a break.

About an hour later, my mom, rest her soul, came up the stairs and handed me a package. It was a 50th birthday present for me from my faraway friend in South Carolina. It was a beautiful crystal and silver cross. How perfect and in perfect timing – His timing.

The Anchor

I have a family history of panic attack disorder. I don't take kindly to medical procedures of any kind; however, I needed to have one. Two days before my procedure where I needed to undergo anesthesia (not my favorite), my youngest had some type of allergic reaction and wound up in an emergency clinic herself.

Thankfully, she was fine, but I was not. I was beyond freaked out about having to go under; what if something happened to her – who would take care of her?

Reaching out to my spirit mate, he was there for me; however, on the day of the procedure, I didn't get a response to my text to him. How could I go into surgery without hearing from my best friend? God spoke to me loud and clear on that morning at 5:00 a.m.

I was ready to cancel the procedure, never having been this frightened in all my life. I clearly heard God reassure me – "Do you really think I would let anything happen to you?" It was so clear and audible; it was not something I could deny.

Suddenly, I felt something like an anchor tether me upward toward him. I knew HE was the one I needed to lean on and I needed to trust.

The lesson for me this unforgettable day was to lean on and depend on no man when God is your main supply. Whether it be love, comfort or support, He is the one on which you can always depend.

Look Up and Then Look Down

At the florist, picking up my daughter's corsage for her prom, I was thinking (again) why don't I have a life partner; it's been years. There was a saying hand painted on the wall – "A dream is a wish your heart makes." I looked down, and in front of me there was a penny and, yes, it was heads up.

Make a Wish: Take a Chance on Love

One day about two years ago, I went to an outdoor live music event in my wonderful town here on Long Island. As I was walking along the boardwalk, I had a strong intuitive feeling which compelled me to turn around and go the other way. Then, just as strongly, I felt compelled to move up front (something I never do – I'm a wallflower at heart) and get closer to the band. I was always living life on the fray, staying back. This always bothered me about myself, but this night I felt compelled to move up front. I listened to the little voice inside me and reluctantly went up front – also known as "out of my comfort zone."

I struck up a conversation with a man there in front of the band, and when it was time to go home, I somehow took on being bold. Completely out of character for me, I asked him if he'd like to meet me there again the following week to listen to another band; he agreed. I took his phone number and we began to date. Maybe we were supposed to meet or maybe, just maybe, I needed to learn how to be seen – authentically and for who I am.

Sometimes God nudges us out of our comfort zone – not for the reasons we think – but because we have a life lesson to learn or a blessing to earn.

One day this gent and I went to my favorite place in the world, The Vanderbilt Mansion. There is a wishing well there. I threw a coin over my shoulder and made a delightful wish (I won't divulge). When we went to go and look for the coin, it was nowhere to be found. It wasn't on the floor, it wasn't in the well; for goodness sake, it landed right inside the pot hanging in the center of the wishing well.

However, my wish didn't come true that day or even in the months following. Things didn't work out with this gent, but a short while later on down the road, someone would come into my life and into my world at the exact same moment my mom began her journey home to heaven a few short months ago.

Coincidence? I think not. God was good and gracious enough to send me someone to help ease my way through the loss of my mom. Not only was she my mom, but I was her caregiver and she lived with me. After many relationships which were not good for me, God honored my wish with this man. I took him to the wishing well and, yes, he kissed me there.

I was struck by fear and made every excuse in the book not to get close to him; I was anxious and afraid of a future upset which hadn't even occurred– I was afraid of falling in love again and I was petrified of getting hurt, one more time.

Only thing is, he went above and beyond to show me differently. The gift in this relationship was the awareness I gained about what was possible for me from a man.

After many hurtful relationships, I didn't even have the remotest idea a man could treat me with so much adoration and affection; the way he looked at me was genuine, authentic, and priceless. I had never known this as a possibility. ***To him it was a given; to me it was a gift.***

The story doesn't end here, however; there's a plot twist. He entered into our new relationship without having rectified the past. Combined with growing, strong feelings for me and seeing what was possible with a healthy life partner and partnership with me, his confusion grew. He's also relocating to North Carolina, and in this moment, it has ended.

It was the shortest yet sweetest, most joyful, and life-lesson learning relationship I had ever had. Although it was filled with unfinished business from the past, it showed potential for a powerful partnership in the future.

Sad but true, each being is here to take this journey one step (or three) at a time. Sometimes we meet the right person at the absolutely wrong time. Other times, our encounters with others are brief and powerful, yet fleeting.

They enter your life to shine a light on something and offer it to you as a gift; while we, on the other hand, unbeknownst to us, were a gift and contribution to them, as well. One more stepping stone on the journey toward healing and wholeness, we were a piece of their puzzle called life, as they were one to us.

There are no wrong steps, no wrong turns, just an ever-forward, free-flowing series of events. Some stones in our pathways are smaller while others require giant leaps to travel across; each one, however, is just as significant as the other no matter how big or how small.

The journey is a pathway made up of a whole; no step is inconsequential and no leap of faith too small.

Endings or Beginnings: Your Choice

Coming on the heels of losing my mom and packing up my youngest to leave the nest and go away to college, I face another choice. Do I look at this as one more loss and another ending or do I view it as a new beginning?

The choice is always ours and while some days are better – much better – than others, I can honestly say I've been through enough and know enough to say this time I'll work hard on waiting to see what unfolds. I don't do well in situations where I don't know what the ending will be. (I love spoiler alerts!).

Maybe I'll relocate too or maybe God has other plans for me; only He knows.

Funny thing, as I went for a walk on the boardwalk recently and bumped into a neighbor, he asked me now that my youngest has left the nest, why don't I downsize and maybe move to North Carolina!

Interesting, curious, intriguing and amusing all rolled into one. I actually am traveling to North Carolina this fall.

One thing is for sure, however, this time I'll just have to learn to sit back and wait - once again in my life - until next time,

When God Nods

APPENDIX
THE LESSONS OF LOVE
AND THE BLESSINGS

Oh so much, probably enough to fill another book, but here is the condensed version:

- Intuition – my intuition was screaming at me to pull away from this man because his past was incomplete; it was so loud, it was audible, but my grief clouded my judgment. I learned not to ignore my intuition and to quiet and still my mind.

- I was telling myself a story that went something like this – without parents and without a partner in my life, surely I would wither up and die, and I couldn't take care of myself. I learned not only could I take care of myself, but I also wanted a man to take care of me too when I needed it. I learned I didn't have to prove to society that I was so tough and independent, but I didn't have to give up my autonomy either. I want both; I deserve both – to be able to care for myself and be cared for (for good reasons) by another human being and, yes, a man. That's sweet.

- To let go of the unknown outcomes – this was a hard sell; I'm nosy, I need to know how, when, where, and why. Letting go of the unknown, I took on, "I trust the outcome will always be for my higher good. God is fully supporting me." This works wonders for the panic and fear which often times drives my mind. Hmmm, the possibility of falling in love with the unknown – anything great can happen at any given time.

- To speak my truth, ask for what I need, and honor myself while being a contribution to another; As long as I speak my truth and do so with compassion and power, I get to live my life as I see fit and as I deserve.

- Present moment living – what a struggle for me, someone who always needs to know what's next. I have such a busy mind. I learned through meditation I can heal my busy brain and I can share my testimony with others on how it is helping me work through panic, change, transition, and fear. It's a struggle and a practice, but oh so very worth it.

- Loving myself the same way I love my children – whoa, there's a stretch. This was an important lesson, one which I am only on Chapter One on. I am learning to love myself without thinking about it – without any reason, just because! No silly affirmations or positive self-talk, just because – wow, that's freedom! – and it's unconditional at its best.

- Letting go – for real – I learned about the deeper meaning of letting go; I could let go of working so damn hard to try and "win" the love, affection, adoration, and attention from a man and just "allow" the right man to come in and do it naturally; just allow it. I am simply "allowing" the right man to win my love and affection instead of me fighting so hard to win his. I am already loved and adored in my own right, just by being me. Pulling away and not trying to chase/win/hold on to this feels freeing. After all, what's not to love?

- Detaching to attach – in order to truly get close to someone, it's necessary to detach from their silly human stuff, as well as your own, so you can attach to their heart and soul.

- Hi, my name is Ann and I can be a control freak – Letting go, but...but...but... I need to control the outcome so it's safest for me. Letting go of control of how other people reacted, of my expectations, of the outcome and of not knowing – just simply repeating, "I am fully supported and the best possible outcome for my highest good is available to me," is crucial in my healing and navigating this life, especially when it comes to men and relationships. There's a place for anger, self-expression, forgiveness of self and others and stepping into the possibility of being carefree when you just loosen the reins a little bit.

- Fear – here's a big inquiry: On the subject of fear - Many losses for me in a short period of time; fear came back to grip me. The harder I tried to fight fear, the bigger it got. Fear didn't come out to harm me; it came out to love me; what a concept. Think about this for a moment. Fear came to deliver a message to me, and, until I was ready to listen and accept the message, it wasn't going to go away any time soon.

- Fear can be a debilitating and unreasonable enemy, but if we take its power away and break it down into love, we can see how fear can express what's not working, what not to do next time; it's time to move upward, onward, and forward. So while fear may seem debilitating, maybe just maybe, if we view it as love and not as the enemy, we can recreate it as a special messenger. We can thank it for doing its job, for loving us so completely it wants to protect us, and it's up to us to discern when it's necessary, when it's not, and when it's needed.

- When I recognized what I was fearing was something I did not want to happen, I could then take action to prevent it. What a powerful and painful lesson to learn – to take fear and recreate it into action rather than sitting still in fear, I could take action steps and choose my own path.

- Choice – At any given moment, I could choose. I could choose this or that; I could choose positive or negative, I could choose to allow grief to do its job. I could choose to move onward, upward, and forward or stay stagnant, or even choose to simply stay still and allow what I was feeling in order to recreate it.

- His will for your life – God removed this relationship from me because it wasn't His will for my life; He has something better planned. I just don't see it yet. I had to recreate anger at God for giving me something which felt so good and then taking it away, and changing it into deep, authentic gratitude to God for giving me something so good (even if for a short while) with a divine message attached to it when I needed it most. This, along with forgiveness of self and others all brings you to the glorious bliss of freedom. Gratitude to God for removing a relationship from me which wasn't for my highest good when I wasn't strong enough to remove it on my own; one which was not intended for a daughter of His in that moment, time, and space. Freedom from anger and sadness, and most of all the toxic effects on your body as a result of these things. It's okay to feel angry and sad, but it's not okay to stay there. So be it; amen! This man handed me a golden orb of shining light; here's my gift to you – this is how you should be treated by a man - not as a bonus, but as a given. A precious gift I won't let remain unopened and I won't be returning any time soon.

- Trust me when I tell you, when you hold onto something which is not God's will for your life – you will struggle. When you surrender it and give it up to Him, He will move mountains to put in place the bountiful and beautiful blessings which are your inherent birth right. How can He fill up your cup if it's overflowing with angst, anger, and sludge? You and only you can empty the glass so as it appears neither half full nor half empty, but to allow for Him to fill it up to overflowing.

- Winning the game – for me, "winning" love and affection was the coveted game. Here's what I learned (hopefully it will shave years off of your quest to "win" at something).*Sometimes winning is learning when to stop playing a losing game.*

Listen to God's calling upon your life and use God's greatest gift wisely - the power of choice (free will). When you combine these two things in order to create your best life yet, you cannot help but notice each and every time…

When God Nods

ABOUT THE AUTHOR

Ann Agueli is a spiritual writer, ghostwriter, author, and web writer. Her heartfelt passion and enlightening experiences as a believer in creation and its creator led her on a mission. She feels called to share divine inspiration and transformational insights through her writing.

Visit Ann at www.theinspiredlivingnetwork.com to check out all her inspirational and transformational books and services or to contact her for life coaching in spiritual and relationship matters. She has another book being published: Transformational Journaling for Mind, Body, Spirit coming soon, as well as a chapter in a compilation book entitled, "The Peacemakers."

Watch for these at www.theinspiredlivingnetwork.com and Amazon.com.

Ann also owns Inspire Content, www.inspirecontent.com, where she uses her creative talents and her heart for helping others to handle writing projects from content consulting to content creation. Content is the connection and she is the bridge. She can help you to emotionally engage with your audience, and her writing makes a difference - one word at a time.

Ann has another award-winning book entitled, "Joy-Full Journaling for the Caregiver's Spirit: A Transformational Workbook." It is filled with inspirational quotes, transformative exercises, and powerful "I AM" affirmations. You can find her caregivers book on Amazon or her website: www.inspirecaregivers.com

Her caregivers Facebook page is found at: www.facebook.com/inspirecaregivers

"I did not choose writing; writing chose me.
Writing is my soul mate."
~ Ann Agueli "Soul Proprietor"

FOR MORE INSPIRATION

For more inspiration, please visit
www.theinspiredlivingnetwork.com.

Also, www.inspirecaregivers.com and sign up for my mailing
list; there are events, articles, resources, caregiver-of-the-month
opportunities and so much more.

Check out my award-winning book:

Joy-Full Journaling for the Caregiver's Spirit: A Transformational
Workbook

http://www.inspirecaregivers.com/product/joy-full-journaling-for-
the-caregivers-spirit-a-transformational-workbook/

I'm available for speaking engagements as well as teaching journaling
to caregivers

Visit my Facebook Page:
https://www.facebook.com/inspirecaregivers/?ref=aymt_homepage
_panel

For all your content creation needs, visit my website:

www.inspirecontent.com

Content is the connection, I am the bridge;
I can engage, enlighten, and inform your audiences turning your
readers into inspired action takers.

Made in the USA
Charleston, SC
28 November 2016